Globalization and International Development

Globalization and International Development
Critical Issues of the 21st Century

Sisay Asefa
Editor

2010

W.E. Upjohn Institute for Employment Research
Kalamazoo, Michigan

Library of Congress Cataloging-in-Publication Data

Globalization and international development : critical issues of the 21st century /
Sisay Asefa, editor.
 p. cm.
 Includes index.
 ISBN-13: 978-0-88099-366-1 (pbk. : alk. paper)
 ISBN-10: 0-88099-366-9 (pbk. : alk. paper)
 ISBN-13: 978-0-88099-367-8 (hbk. : alk. paper)
 ISBN-10: 0-88099-367-7 (hbk. : alk. paper)
 1. Globalization—Economic aspects. 2. Economic development. 3. International
trade. 4. International finance. 5. Economic assistance. 6. Poverty. I. Sisay Asefa,
1950-
 HF1359.G58277 2010
 338.91—dc22
                          2010010285

The facts presented in this study and the observations and viewpoints expressed are
the sole responsibility of the authors. They do not necessarily represent positions of
the W.E. Upjohn Institute for Employment Research.

Cover design by Alcorn Publication Design.
Index prepared by Diane Worden.
Printed in the United States of America.
Printed on recycled paper.

Contents

Acknowledgments

This book contains chapters based on presentations made at the 44th annual Werner Sichel Economics Lecture-Seminar Series, hosted by the Department of Economics at Western Michigan University during the academic year 2007–2008. The series was made possible through the financial support of the W.E. Upjohn Institute for Employment Research and Western Michigan University. The series is named for Professor Werner Sichel, who retired in 2005 following 45 years of teaching economics at Western Michigan University. A Fulbright Scholar, Dr. Sichel is the author and editor of 18 publications in economics, including *The State of Economic Science: Views of Six Nobel Laureates,* which he edited and which was published by the Upjohn Institute.

In directing the lecture series and in preparing this book, I am most grateful to the chapter authors: without their cooperation, this book would not have been possible. I am also grateful to my colleagues in the Department of Economics at Western Michigan University for their assistance in organizing the lecture series. In particular, I am thankful to the members of the economics department lectures committee for the 2007–2008 academic year: Dr. Michael Ryan, Dr. Ed Van Wesep, and Dr. Randall Eberts, president of the Upjohn Institute. Finally, I am especially thankful to the Upjohn Institute for its cosponsorship of the series and for its excellent editorial services during the publication of this book.

1
Introduction

Sisay Asefa
Western Michigan University

This collection is based on the papers presented at the 2007–2008 Werner Sichel Lecture-Seminar series held at Western Michigan University. These papers address the issue of globalization with a special emphasis on its impact on poverty. The dawning of the twenty-first century is a propitious time to examine this issue. Advances in transportation and, especially, telecommunications have imposed virtual synchronicity on nations. Information and communication flows are virtually instantaneous. However, wide differences in cultures, political systems, languages, and ethnicities impose barriers to optimal use of the technological advances that have occurred. Extreme variation in the international distributions of wealth, income, and poverty remain as enormous social problems to be addressed.

The general perspective of the economists who have contributed to this collection of papers is that expanding "flows" between countries is the appropriate direction for economies both in terms of accelerating growth and reducing inequalities. These flows include international trade and capital, migration, remittances, and foreign aid. But in addition to these hard commodities and dollars, there are flows of ideas, knowledge, and technical assistance. Of course, as one of the authors reminds us, appropriate intellectual property rights need to be enforced concomitantly with the flow of ideas and knowledge.

The book begins with the chapter by Ian Goldin and Kenneth A. Reinert, who explore how globalization in the structure of trade and capital flows in its various forms (foreign direct investment, portfolio investment, and commercial bank lending) affect poverty. They also discuss the effect of foreign aid, international migration, and remittances, including the global flow of ideas in the form of knowledge and information.

Goldin and Reinert offer a historical view of globalization and describe three distinct stages of modern globalization, the first of which dates back to approximately 1870. In discussing the historical relationship among these three stages, they note that globalization and global poverty can be either positively or negatively related to each other. From 1870 to 1929 and the beginning of the Great Depression, globalization and global poverty increased together. However, the retreat from globalization during the Great Depression and World War II was accompanied by a continued increase in global poverty. A key public policy challenge facing humankind, they say, is to eliminate this still-prominent level of extreme poverty.

Goldin and Reinert write that while globalization has the potential to be a vehicle for shared growth, prosperity, and reductions in poverty, that potential is not yet being adequately realized. They conclude their chapter with several recommendations to improve the effects of globalization.

Chapter 3 by Susan Pozo emphasizes that globalization through migration is a powerful global force with potential benefits for individuals and community out-migrants. Pozo discusses the role of current remittances and how these forms of capital inflows to developing countries have the potential to reduce sudden stops or shocks. In other words, countries that experience large inflows of remittances appear less vulnerable to economic recessions from sudden withdrawal of capital, assuming these inflows are motivated by altruism. Altruism inflows to developing countries are countercyclical, reducing the damage that foreign investors may impart when they perceive sudden shock in poor performance and withdraw financial resources.

Pozo reminds us that free flows of capital where it is abundant should earn low returns to areas where it is abundant and earn higher returns where it scarce, as in developing countries. Globalization driven both by trade and capital flows generally leads to a positive sum outcome, and not a zero sum game. The same idea is true for migration, which involves the flow of human capital. She concludes by arguing that despite political impediments to labor migration, migration and other forms of globalization driven by technical changes, trade, and capital flows are likely to lead to growth of the world economy with the potential to reduce global poverty.

Chapter 4 by Joseph Joyce explores the impact of globalization on income and wealth inequality. Joyce reviews the evidence on the determinants of disparities in per capita income with a focus on the institutions that affect globalization. He implies that globalization can be better managed to benefit the poor. The United States and other industrial countries have a major responsibility to help promote globalization with a human face. In particular, the greatest challenge of global poverty and inequality exists in Africa and the Middle East in the coming century, with symptoms that pose serious global challenges: deadly conflicts, human rights abuses, terrorism, rebellion, and dictatorships. Overcoming these challenges, Joyce says, will make a significant contribution to globalization and result in global peace, stability, poverty alleviation, and human security.

Linda Tesar, in Chapter 5, examines how the composition of global and financial flows has changed and the role of the markets in the process. She discusses the history of financial flows and their responses to the Washington Consensuses I and II. Washington I refers to policy recommendations by Washington-based global institutions, such as the International Monetary Fund, the World Bank, and the U.S. Treasury, which recommended to developing countries to liberalize market prices by "getting prices right." This policy later proved too limited and led to the Washington II Consensus of "getting institutions right."

Tesar shows the change in composition for global financial flows to emerging markets during the post–financial crisis period. External development finance is now more likely to take the form of a sale of domestic assets, with control rights shifting to the acquiring firm, which is a natural response to weak institutions in emerging markets. While control of foreign subsidiaries allows both for capital flow and for protection of property rights of the acquiring firm, it is not a substitute for strong institutions that would extend to all firms in emerging markets. The upshot is this: getting institutions right is critical to attracting FDI in developing economies.

In Chapter 6, Lisa Cook investigates the issue of intellectual property rights based on evidence from plant patents from 1977 to 2007 for selected developing countries. She addresses the problem of the provisions of Trade Property Rights Intellectual Protections in developing countries. With weak capacity to protect intellectual property rights at home, low-income countries are robbed of their innovations, including cultural and historical property asset rights. Cook explores the question of how a developing country may respond to the challenge of greater intellectual property protection, and whether foreign patent offices have become complements and substitutes for domestic patent offices.

The book concludes with Chapter 7 by Hadi Esfahani, who asks whether we as a society and as individuals are developing the right skills and procedures to deal with the challenges of new global opportunities. To address this question, Esfahani discusses previous trends in globalization, which have consisted of greater integration of world markets with the help of technological progress and improved governance across countries. He then turns to future trends in globalization, and says that policy reforms are unlikely to make countries uniform in terms of governance and regulation, but they will bring about greater harmony. Esfahani concludes his chapter by discussing the types of skills necessary to compete in a future global economy.

One of the goals of this lecture series is that reading these thought-provoking papers will stimulate action. It will stimulate the reader to search for additional resources on the issues raised. It will stimulate the reader to bring a more well-grounded understanding to debates about globalization. It will stimulate readers to confront xenophobic proscriptions to let other countries solve their own problems. Like many aspects of progress, globalization has great potential and has its downsides. The goal of collecting papers that analyze issues of globalization is to inform readers about both.

2
Can Globalization Help?

Ian Goldin
Oxford University

Kenneth A. Reinert
George Mason University

Globalization broadly refers to the expansion of worldwide linkages within and increasing interdependence of human activity in the economic, social, cultural, political, technological, and even biological spheres. The areas in which globalization operates can interact with one another. For instance, while HIV/AIDS is a biological phenomenon, it interacts with economic, social, cultural, political, and technological forces at global, regional, national, and community levels. The relationship between globalization and development is not well understood, and disagreement regarding this relationship abounds. Globalization is, to many, the best means of bringing prosperity to the greatest number of people all around the world. For others, it represents an important cause of global poverty.

The five economic dimensions of globalization examined here are trade, finance, aid, migration, and ideas. Whereas trade is the exchange of goods and services among the countries of the world, capital flows involve the exchange of assets or financial instruments among these countries. Foreign aid involves the transfer of loans and grants among countries, as well as technical assistance or capacity building. Migration takes place when people move between countries, either temporarily or permanently, to seek education and employment or to escape adverse political environments. Ideas represent the broadest globalization phenomenon. They involve the generation and international transmission of intellectual constructs in areas such as technology, management, or governance.

One can hope that these dimensions of economic globalization would contribute to development and poverty alleviation, and this is

5

indeed often the case. In other instances, however, the link between globalization and development breaks down. As we will argue here, there are no statements regarding the relationship between globalization and development that are both simple and accurate. Rather, statements regarding this relationship are necessarily complex if they are to be accurate.[1]

A HISTORICAL VIEW

Economic historians date the modern era of globalization to approximately 1870. The period from 1870 to 1914 is often considered to be the birth of the modern world economy, which, by some measures, was as integrated as it is today. Historians have observed that, from the point of view of capital flows, the late 1800s were an extraordinary time.[2] The global integration of capital markets was facilitated by advances in rail and ship transportation and in telegraph communication. European colonial systems were at their highest stages of development, and migration was at a historical high point in relation to the global population of the time.

This first modern stage of globalization was followed by two additional stages, one from the late 1940s to the mid-1970s and another from the mid-1970s to the present. These, however, were preceded by World War I, the Great Depression, and World War II. During these events, many aspects of globalization were reversed as the world experienced increased conflict, nationalism, and patterns of economic autarky. To some extent, then, the second and third modern stages of globalization merely involved regaining lost levels of international integration.

The second modern stage of globalization began at the end of World War II. It was accompanied by a global, economic regime developed by the Bretton Woods Conference of 1944 establishing the International Monetary Fund (IMF), what was to become the World Bank, and the General Agreement on Tariffs and Trade (GATT). This stage of globalization involved an increase in capital flows from the United States, as well as a U.S.-inspired production system that relied on exploiting economies of scale in manufacturing and the advance of U.S.-based multinational enterprises (MNEs).

This second stage also involved some reduction of trade barriers under the auspices of GATT. Developing countries were not highly involved in this liberalization, however. In export products of interest to developing countries (agriculture, textiles, and clothing), a system of nontariff measures in rich countries evolved. Also, a set of key developing countries, especially those in Latin America, pursued import substitution industrialization with their own trade barriers.[3] These developments, along with the Cold War, suppressed the integration of many developing countries into the world trading system.

The third modern stage of globalization began in the late 1970s. This stage followed the demise of monetary relationships developed at the Bretton Woods Conference and involved the emergence of the newly industrialized countries of East Asia, especially Japan, Taiwan (China), and the Republic of Korea. Rapid technological progress, particularly in transportation, communication, and information technology, began to dramatically lower the costs of moving goods, capital, people, and ideas across the globe.[4]

What has been the historical relationship among these three stages of modern globalization and development? A partial view is found in Figure 2.1. This figure combines a single measure of globalization—exports as a percentage of world gross domestic product (GDP)—with a single measure of poverty—the number of extremely dollar poor people—in a time series from 1870 to 1998. What is clear from this figure is that, historically, globalization and global poverty can be either positively related or negatively related to each other. From 1870 through 1929 and the beginning of the Great Depression, globalization (trade) and global poverty increased together. However, the retreat from globalization during the Great Depression and World War II was accompanied by a continued increase in global poverty. This can be seen from the 1950 data in the figure showing that, when exports as a percentage of GDP had declined nearly back to the 1870 level, extreme poverty reached a peak of approximately 1.4 billion persons.

As seen in Figure 2.1, the increase in globalization as measured by trade in the second and third stages of modern globalization has been associated with a gradual decline in extreme poverty to approximately 1.1 billion people. During these stages, globalization and poverty have been negatively associated with each other, albeit mildly so. A key public policy challenge facing humankind is to *eliminate* this still-prominent

Figure 2.1 Trade and Extreme Poverty in Historical Perspective

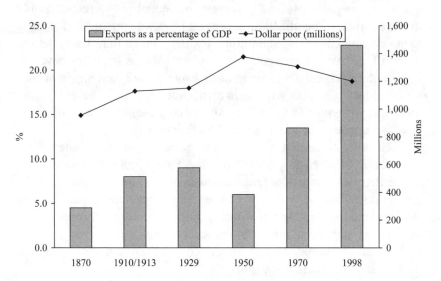

SOURCE: Exports as a percentage of GDP from Ocampo and Martin (2003), based on
Maddison (2001). Dollar poor from Bourguignon and Morrisson (2002) and Chen and
Ravallion (2004).

level of extreme poverty. Understanding how to do this requires a deeper understanding of the links between globalization and poverty.

TRADE

Of all aspects of globalization, international trade is held out as the
great hope for poverty alleviation.[5] Trade can contribute to poverty alleviation by expanding markets, promoting competition, and raising productivity, each of which has the potential to increase the real incomes
of poor people. But it would be a mistake to rely on trade liberalization
alone as a means of reducing poverty.[6] A more comprehensive approach
is needed that addresses multiple economic and social challenges simultaneously and that emphasizes the expansion of poor people's capabili-

ties, especially in the areas of health and education.[7] Nevertheless, trade has some vital roles to play.

Since the mid-1980s, developing countries have increased their global trade exports significantly, even in services where their comparative advantage is typically seen as weak. For various reasons, not the least of which are trade barriers maintained by rich countries, developing country agricultural (primary) exports have been stagnant (see Figure 2.2). There is also a divergence of export experience across developing countries, with Africa's share of world exports declining over time.

International trade is a means of expanding markets, and market expansion can help generate employment and incomes for poor people. Comparisons are often made between the wages of workers in poor-country export industries and the wages of workers in developed countries. In these comparisons, the wages of workers in developing-country export industries often appear to be very low. Consequently, trade has often been identified as poverty worsening. However, the more rele-

Figure 2.2 Nominal Exports of Developing Countries

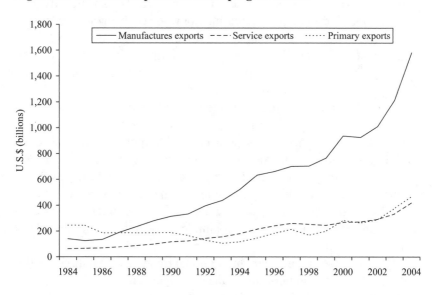

SOURCE: World Bank, World Development Indicators Online.

vant comparison is between the wages of export sector workers with agricultural day laborers, both in the same developing country. Here it can often be seen that the alternative of agricultural day labor is much worse. It is precisely this type of income comparison that draws workers into export industries.[8]

It must be kept in mind that not all export activity is equal from the point of view of raising the incomes of poor people. Exporting can best contribute to poverty alleviation when it supports labor-intensive production, human capital accumulation (both education and health), and technological learning. In addition, the incomes of poor individuals depend on buoyant and sustainable export incomes, which in turn are dependent on export prices.

International trade is also a means of promoting competition, and in many instances, this can help poor people. Increased competition lowers the real costs of both consumption and production. For example, domestic monopolies charge monopoly prices that can be significantly above competitive prices. The competition introduced by imports erodes market power, lowering prices. These procompetitive effects of trade can expand household budgets and lower the costs of production. The latter can have additional employment effects that are advantageous to poor individuals by lowering nonwage costs in labor-intensive production activities. Procompetitive effects can also arise in the case of monopsony power. Here, sellers (small farmers, for example) to the monopsony buyer are able to obtain higher prices for their goods as the buying power of the monopsonist is eroded.

There is some evidence that international trade can promote productivity in a country, and it is possible that productivity increases can in turn support the incomes of poor people.[9] Exports of all types or in all countries cannot generate positive productivity effects, but in certain instances they can. Export postures can place the exporting firms in direct contact with discerning international customers, facilitating upgrading processes. There is no consensus within international economics on the extent of these upgrading effects, but they are present in some cases.[10]

There are occasions when international trade can have direct health and safety impacts on poor individuals—impacts that can be beneficial or detrimental. Perhaps most importantly, improving the health outcomes of poor people usually involves imports of medical products. It is simply not possible for most small, developing countries to produce the entire range of even basic medical supplies, no less more advanced medical equipment and pharmaceuticals. However, many developing countries import large amounts of weaponry and export sexual services, both of which can have dramatically negative outcomes for the health and safety of poor individuals.[11] In addition, the production processes of some export industries can adversely affect the health of workers in those industries, and a small but important amount of trade involves hazardous waste dumping.

CAPITAL FLOWS

Private capital flows are an important resource for developing countries. They augment domestic savings and can contribute to investment, growth, financial sector development, and technology transfer. However, there is also substantial evidence that capital flows entail potential costs that are both much larger than in the case of trade and disproportionately carried by the poor. Additionally, it has become clear that not all capital flows are the same in their benefit and cost characteristics. For these reasons, the cost and benefit characteristics of distinct types of capital flows must be considered in some detail.[12] Here we distinguish among foreign direct investment, equity portfolio investment, bond finance, and commercial bank lending.

The financial markets involved in equity portfolio investment, bond finance, and commercial bank lending are characterized by a number of market failures. In normal circumstances, these imperfections tend to contribute to a certain amount of market volatility, as shown in Figure 2.3. Under certain circumstances that are not fully understood (but are particularly important in emerging economies), they can lead to full-blown financial crises. Imperfections in financial markets appear to be particularly problematic when commercial banks in developing countries are given access to short-term, foreign lending sources.[13] The resulting problems have three causes. First, systems of financial intermediation in developing countries tend to rely heavily on the banking sector, while other types of financial intermediation typically are being underdeveloped. Second, developing countries have been encouraged

Figure 2.3 Nominal Flows of Aid, FDI, Portfolio Investment, and Remittances to Developing Countries

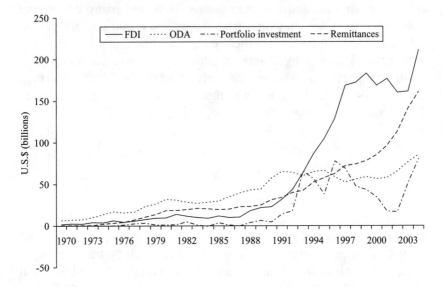

SOURCE: World Bank, World Development Indicators Online.

to liberalize domestic financial markets, sometimes before systems of prudential bank regulation and management are put in place. Third, developing countries have sometimes prematurely liberalized their capital accounts.[14] Consequently, care must be taken in managing evolving financial systems and their access to international capital flows.

Foreign Direct Investment

Foreign direct investment (FDI) can have positive impacts on poverty by creating employment, improving technology and human capital, and promoting competition. Not all kinds of FDI contribute in this way, however, and some can adversely impact certain dimensions of poverty through unsafe working conditions and environmental degradation. Nevertheless, as it pertains to poverty alleviation, FDI is the most promising category of capital flows.[15] As can be seen in Figure 2.3, these flows have risen substantially in recent years.

Many developing countries lack access to the technologies available in developed countries, and hosting MNEs from developed countries is one way to potentially gain access to that technology. There are limits to technology transfer, however. First, MNEs will employ the technology that most suits *their* strategic needs and not the development needs of host countries. For example, MNEs can employ processes that are much more capital intensive than would be desired on the basis of host-country employment considerations.[16] Second, there is a strong tendency for MNEs to conduct their research and development in their home bases rather than in host countries.[17]

Despite these general limitations, in some important cases, MNEs do transfer technology and establish significant relationships with host-country suppliers via backward linkages. If foreign MNE begins to source inputs locally rather than by importing them, the host country can gain a number of important benefits. First, employment can increase since the sourced inputs represent new production. Second, production technologies can be better adapted to local conditions since suppliers are more likely to employ labor-intensive processes. Third, the MNE can transfer state-of-the-art business practices and technologies to the local suppliers. Fourth, it is possible that the local suppliers can coalesce into a spatial cluster that supports innovation and upgrading.[18]

Another avenue through which MNEs can positively affect host economies is through "spillovers" to other sectors of these economies. The evidence to date suggests that such spillovers do occur in some circumstances and can be significant. However, in the words of Blomström and Sjöholm (1999), they are not "guaranteed, automatic, or free." What determines whether positive technology spillovers will occur? Many factors are involved, and these include host country policies, MNE behavior, and industry characteristics. One key factor is the capacity of local firms to absorb foreign technologies. Blomström and Kokko (2003) suggest that learning is a key capacity that is responsive to various host country policies, and evidence presented in Tsang, Nguyen, and Erramilli (2004) in the case of Vietnam supports this view.

There is some evidence that MNEs in Africa offer higher wages than domestic firms (see te Velde and Morrissey [2003]). This effect is more predominant for skilled than unskilled workers. FDI can therefore have differential impacts that exclude unskilled workers. This can result in what te Velde (2001) refers to as the "low-income low-skill trap." All of these considerations point to the role of basic education and skills development in making the most of FDI for poverty alleviation.[19]

The low-income countries as a whole are largely excluded from global FDI flows. For example, in 2002, low-income countries received only 2 percent of total FDI flows, with nearly half of this going to India and Vietnam alone. For these countries, exclusion from this dimension of globalization is a long-term concern.

Equity Portfolio Investment

There is evidence that capital inflows in the form of equity portfolio investment might be more beneficial than both bond finance and commercial bank lending. For example, Reisen and Soto (2001) have examined the impact of all four capital inflows considered here on growth for a sample of 44 countries. They find that FDI, considered above, did indeed have a positive impact on economic growth. The most positive growth impact, however, came from equity portfolio flows. Bond finance, considered below, did not have any impact on growth, and commercial bank lending, also considered below, had a negative impact. These results suggest that equity inflows, along with FDI, could play an especially positive role in growth, development, and poverty alleviation.

Why can equity portfolio investment play a positive role in growth and development, at least under some circumstances? Rousseau and Wachtel (2000) summarize research on this question with four possibilities: 1) equity portfolio inflows are an important source of funds for developing countries; 2) the development of equity markets helps to provide an exit mechanism for venture capitalists, and this increases entrepreneurial activity; 3) portfolio inflows assist developing countries to move from short-term finance to longer-term finance and help to finance investment in projects that have economies of scale; and 4) the development of equity markets provides an informational mechanism evaluating the performance of domestic firms and can help provide incentives to managers to perform well.

With regard to volatility, there is some evidence that institutional investors managing equity flows are less likely than banks to engage in herd and contagion behavior.[20] However, in general, equity markets are underdeveloped in much of the developing world. For example, nearly the entire net portfolio equity inflows into Sub-Saharan Africa are accounted for by one country alone: South Africa. The World Bank (2004) summarizes the features of developing-country equity markets as follows:

> Market capitalization as a share of GDP in low-income countries is about one-sixth of that in high-income countries . . . Stock exchanges in developing countries also tend to lag technologically behind developed markets. Technology plays a major role in the trading, clearance, and settlement processes; problems in those areas can discourage sophisticated investors. Institutions that supervise and support the operation of the stock exchange also tend to be weaker in developing countries. (p. 95)

The development of equity markets in low- and middle-income countries is more complex than it might first appear, however. This is due to the increased globalization of financial services. Observers have pointed to a set of domestic factors as being particularly important in equity market development. These factors include sound macroeconomic policies, minimal degrees of technology, legal systems that protect shareholders, and open financial markets. However, as pointed out by Claessens, Klingebiel, and Schmukler (2002), these are precisely the factors that tend to promote the "migration" of equity exchange out of developing countries to the major exchanges in financial capital of developed countries. This migration process complicates standard notions of equity market development. Steil (2001) has argued that the way forward is to link local markets with global markets. However, there might remain medium-sized firms with local information needs that could benefit from some kind of domestic or regional equity market. This is an area that requires urgent attention for the development of novel approaches.

Bond Finance and Commercial Bank Lending

In the minds of the financial world, there are significant differences between portfolio equity investment and debt. This shows up in the fact that, in the case of bankruptcy, debt is given priority over equity. This tends to support the preference for debt over equity in markets, a preference that appears to be misplaced from a development and poverty alleviation perspective. With regard to commercial bank lending, Dobson and Hufbauer (2001) note that "bank lending may be more prone to run than portfolio capital, because banks themselves are highly leveraged, and they are relying on the borrower's balance sheet to ensure repayment" (p. 47). The World Bank (2001) notes that "incentives are key to limiting undue risk-taking and fraudulent behavior in the management and supervision of financial intermediaries—especially banks that are prone to costly failure" (p. 3).

What can be done to support the safe development of banking sectors in low-income countries? Some of the necessary steps can be thought of in terms of information, institutions, and incentives. With regard to information, it is important for banks to embrace internationally sanctioned accounting and auditing procedures and to make the results of these assessments available to the public. In the case of institutions or the rules of the "banking game," risk management practices (both credit and currency) must be sufficiently stringent, and prudential regulation systems must be well developed. With regard to currency risk, the World Bank (2004) notes that "particular care should be taken to ensure that foreign-currency liabilities are appropriately hedged" (p. 30).[21] These information and institutional safeguards are no small task and inevitably cannot be achieved in the short term. Consequently, they should be buttressed with incentive measures in the form of market-friendly taxes on banking capital inflows. For example, Eichengreen (1999) argues that "banks borrowing abroad should be required to put up additional noninterest-bearing reserves with the central bank" (p. 117). Such taxes on short-term capital inflows in the form of variable deposit requirements appear to be important to prevent destabilizing episodes of overborrowing.[22]

To summarize, debt flows in the form of bond finance and commercial bank lending appear to have different properties than equity flows in the form of FDI and portfolio equity investment. They are more prone to the imperfect behaviors that characterize financial markets and do not appear to have positive growth effects as large as those associated with equity flows. Consequently, utilization of debt finance must be cautious and sufficiently hedged against exchange rate risks.

AID

It has been relatively recently that governments began to provide financial and technical assistance to foreign countries. The purpose of this assistance has varied and has included geopolitical objectives, stimulating economic development, ameliorating poverty, promoting political outcomes, and ensuring civil stability. Although foreign aid is often visualized in terms of financial "handouts" by rich countries to the world's poorest inhabitants, the truth is significantly more complex. Indeed, contrary to popular perception, low-income countries generally receive less than half of total aid flows. Much of the remainder is made up by flows to middle-income countries, and some high-income countries of strategic interest receive significant amounts of assistance.

Foreign aid, or official development assistance (ODA), as it is technically known, is composed of a wide range of financial and nonfinancial instruments used in support of growth and poverty-reduction efforts. The transfer of financial resources is an important part of development assistance, but finance is only one of the instruments used to support development. Nonfinancial forms of assistance include tangible grants of machinery or equipment and less tangible contributions such as the provision of technical analysis, advice, or capacity building, including trade-related capacity building. Such forms of assistance are vital, especially in environments where finance is not likely to contribute to poverty reduction, such as early in postconflict situations or where institutions are particularly weak.

As is evident in Figure 2.3, since the 1990s, FDI and portfolio flows have dwarfed the historically recent flow of aid. For example, development aid in 2005 (US$106 billion) totaled only slightly over one-third of FDI in developing countries (US$281 billion). In terms of historical availability, flows of aid saw an initial rise from 1945 to 1960 but then increased only slowly from the 1960s until around 1990. From then until 2001, they dropped to only 0.2 percent of the GDP of high-income countries. In the last four or so years, this trend has been reversed, with ODA reaching a record high in 2005 and many countries committing themselves to doubling aid budgets by 2010. But only 5 of the 22 high-income countries of the OECD's Development Assistance Committee that pledged 0.7 percent of their GDP to foreign aid actually met this goal as of 2005.

In 2000, the Millennium Development Goals signaled a renewed push for increased aid flows and better aid effectiveness, and there has been significant recent progress in increasing the impact of aid. Indeed, the estimated poverty-reduction productivity of ODA is significantly better than it was in the early 1990s (Collier and Dollar 2004).[23] When all aid is lumped together, some analyses have found no clear relationship between aid and growth or poverty reduction (see, for example, Boone [1996]). But not all aid is aimed directly at poverty reduction, nor has aid always been provided in ways that will maximize growth. Moreover, because aid is often provided to help countries cope with external shocks, even if aid is reasonably well designed and allocated, the positive impact of such aid may be obscured by the magnitude of the shocks. Disaster relief, for example, is not aimed directly at long-term poverty reduction, and thus it is no surprise that such aid is not correlated with that result.[24] However, it does achieve its goal of helping to avert famine or assisting countries to recover from natural disasters.

Donors initially placed too much emphasis on the role of what were often isolated projects, neglecting the quality of the overall country environment for growth, a mistake that adjustment or (policy-based) aid was intended to overcome. Additionally, as mentioned above, aid was sometimes allocated for purely strategic reasons, with growth and poverty reduction in these cases being distinct secondary concerns, if they were concerns at all. Given this diversity of motives, it is not surprising that aid did not always have the hoped-for effects on growth and poverty reduction.

The adjustment programs that came into their own in partial response to the macroeconomic imbalances of the 1970s had their own problems. Donors incorrectly believed that conditionality on loans and grants could substitute for country ownership. Too often, governments receiving aid were not truly committed to reforms. Moreover, neither donors nor governments focused sufficiently on poverty in designing the adjustment programs. In many countries, donors underestimated the importance of governance, institutional reforms, and social investments. Prescriptions for reform were too formulaic, ignoring the central need for country specificity. As a result, weak governance and institutions reduced the amount of productivity growth and poverty reduction that could result from the macroeconomic reforms.

During the 1990s, a rethinking of development models and the role of aid began. This was facilitated by a combination of four developments. First, the end of the Cold War reduced the geopolitical pressures on aid agencies. Second, there was an increasing recognition of the successes of India, China, and other developing countries that had achieved macro balance and sustained growth while adopting their own particular development models. Third, there was mounting evidence of an apparent failure of orthodox adjustment models adopted by African and other highly indebted countries, as evidenced by the lack of positive growth and poverty outcomes. Finally, there was a growing body of analytic literature that highlighted the importance of the need for a more comprehensive approach to development and wider understanding of poverty, focusing on both human capital (education, health) and physical capital (infrastructure), as well as institutions and participation.[25]

The statistical evidence shows that large-scale financial aid can generally be used effectively for poverty reduction when reasonably good policies are in place.[26] In recent years, donors have increasingly acted on these findings by tailoring support to local needs and circumstances. Thus, the balance of support has moved toward providing large-scale aid to those that can use it well and focusing on knowledge and capacity-building support in other countries. This has been reflected in greater selectivity and coordination in lending, shifting resources toward governance and institutions, emphasizing ownership, and making room for diverse responses to local needs. These new approaches and procedures have begun to pay off. However, it is clear that there is still much to learn: for example, how can countries with very weak governance effectively catalyze and support reforms and institution building?

Should we then use only policy and institutional quality as measures in determining aid flows? This would probably be too rash a conclusion. Research by Clemens, Radelet, and Bhavnani (2004) takes an entirely different approach: instead of focusing on the different policy and institutional characteristics of recipient countries, they focus on the characteristics of different types of aid flows. Importantly, they only consider what they term "short-impact" aid, which includes budget and balance of payments support, infrastructure investments, and aid for

productive sectors such as agriculture and industry. In contrast to previous studies, they find a strong impact of aid on growth (and thus on
poverty reduction, at least to some extent) regardless of institutions and
policies.[27] In light of such evidence, it probably is too soon to call for
substantial reallocations of aid other than of those flows that reflect only
strategic, rather than humanitarian or economic, considerations.

MIGRATION

International migration involves the movement of people, on either
a temporary or permanent basis, among the countries of the world
economy. Throughout human history, these changes of residence have
helped to alleviate human suffering, enhance technological progress,
and promote cultural exchange. As of 2006, approximately 200 million
people, or 3 percent of the world's population, lived outside their country of birth. Although this percentage is low by historical standards,
international migration has doubled since 1980. Migration continues to
be a key dimension of globalization and development, albeit one that
has complex determinants and outcomes.

A central component of the modern era of globalization that began
in the late nineteenth century was the Age of Mass Migration, described
by Hatton and Williamson (1998). Between 1850 and 1914, approximately 55 million Europeans migrated, most of them unskilled males
who settled in the United States. As Manning (2005) emphasizes, however, the Age of Mass Migration was not just European in nature, with
50 million Chinese and 30 million Indians also migrating (not all vol-
untarily), primarily to serve as unskilled laborers in British colonies in
Africa and the Pacific. Since then, much has changed, with migration
becoming an increasingly elusive escape route from poverty.

High-skilled migrants from developing countries are commonly
trained at substantial costs to the taxpayers of source countries through
public education systems. Their departure thus has profound effects in
the form of what is known as brain drain. Source countries can also
lose tax revenues that migrants would have generated. More importantly, many of the skills sent from less-developed to more-developed
countries are already scarce in source countries. In the case of medi-

cal services, for which more-developed countries have a strong desire and less-developed countries an urgent need, the brain drain can cost lives. In Malawi, for example, HIV/AIDS has reduced the country's life expectancy to under 40 years. Despite this health crisis, the country has lost approximately half its nursing staff to migration. Partly as a result, the rate at which Malawian women die during pregnancy and childbirth has approximately doubled.[28]

The emigration of skilled workers does not always create problems for source countries. In some cases, emigration alerts outside investors to a large or relatively underused skill base of the source country. The success of skilled Indian migrants in the United States, for instance, helped to spur the large inflow of information and communication technology-related FDI to India seen during recent years. Many foreign information and communication technology companies, impressed by the talent working for them outside India, sought equivalently skilled individuals within India as employees in FDI-related facilities. Thus, when the conditions are right, skilled migrants are able to generate networks of investment, trade, and technology transfer that increase the productivity and demand for skills in the home country, while extending the global technology frontier and lowering the cost of products used by billions of people worldwide.

Another potentially compensating benefit of the brain drain is that it tends to increase the demand for skills in the source country by raising the rate of return to education. Some researchers have suggested that, even accounting for the emigration of skilled individuals, the increase in demand for education generated by brain drain may actually increase the number of skilled workers in the population. This is known as brain gain. While brain gain outcomes are possible, they depend on very large responses in the supply of education and training. They are not, therefore, a general outcome of high-skilled migration.

The most easily quantifiable benefit of emigration to source countries is the flow of money, or remittances, sent by migrant workers to their home countries. Recent estimates suggest that the total remittance flow to developing countries now exceeds US$200 billion (see Figure 2.3, which does not quite capture the current value due to data lags in the other series). In a number of countries, remittance inflows are larger than inflows of foreign direct investment and can compose up to 10 percent of national incomes. As is evident in Figure 2.4, such flows can

Figure 2.4 Foreign Remittances, 2003

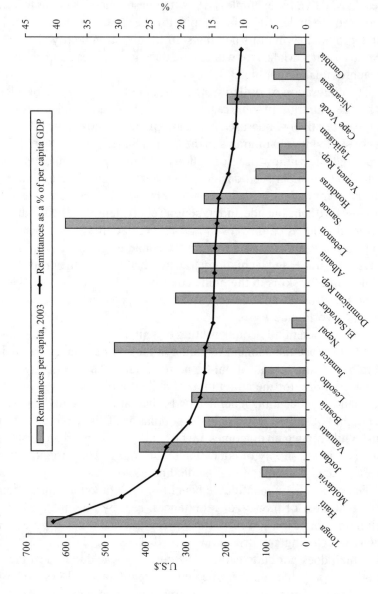

SOURCE: World Bank, World Development Indicators Online.

make a significant difference for families living in poverty in source countries, which is a common reason why communities allow and sometimes even encourage their family members to seek work abroad (see Adams and Page [2005]).

Under the auspices of the World Trade Organization (WTO), the liberalization of services trade has occurred in a number of sectors of interest to developed countries such as finance and telecommunications. The WTO's General Agreement of Trade in Services (GATS) recognizes the temporary movement of natural persons as a way to export certain labor-intensive services such as housekeeping and construction. Given the natural comparative advantage of developing countries in such labor-intensive services, this channel could be of great importance to their trade and development prospects. The WTO protocol on the temporary movement of natural persons, however, is largely limited to the exchange of corporate personnel and is not designed to enhance the delivery of labor-intensive services. This urgently needs to be rectified.

IDEAS

Idea formation and reformation have been and continue to be integral to development processes and policies because, as emphasized by Adelman (2001), development processes are significantly nonlinear and nonunique. Consequently, ideas play a key role in organizing and making sense of development experience and have gone through a number of paradigm shifts. Importantly, the environments to which development ideas respond are increasingly affected by the various processes characterizing globalization. For this reason, the role of ideas in development processes cannot be clearly understood without reference to the various other dimensions of increased global integration.

Ideas are both a powerful influence on development and a key dimension of globalization. Relevant here are three areas of inquiry related to ideas, development, and globalization: 1) the idea of development itself, along with the related issue of the idea of growth; 2) the role of ideas in globalization processes; and 3) the question of ideas for development, along with the related issues of development knowledge management, intellectual property, and learning. We focus here on the last of these, ideas for development, since it has the most relevance to this chapter.

Ideas are codified in the form of knowledge, and knowledge is in many respects a public good. Once an idea has been codified, that knowledge can often be used at low marginal cost, and its use by any one person does not preclude its use by others. This characteristic of knowledge is precisely the hallmark of a public good and suggests that knowledge, like other public goods, will be underprovided by market systems. The challenge, then, is the effective development and management of knowledge, recognizing its (global) public good nature. Knowledge management, a difficult task for firms, is even more daunting for developing countries.

A first element of knowledge management for development is increasing the voice of developing countries and their impoverished citizens.[29] This is an essential ingredient of inclusive globalization and is especially important in global consultation and decision making with direct consequences for the citizens of developing countries. It is also important to enhance developing-country participation in global institutions in order to ensure their legitimacy. The governance of the United Nations (at least at the Security Council level), the World Bank, and the IMF reflects the balance of power 60 years ago.[30] There is widespread recognition of the need for enhancing the participation of developing countries. Although some progress has been made in areas related to program formation, the structural issues of voting rights and board representation remain intractable. It remains, however, as stated by Bhattacharya and Griffith-Jones (2004), "important to go beyond consultation to full representation of developing countries in bodies that deliberate and set international norms and action plans" (p. 205). The principles of transparency, accountability, and good governance that the global institutions advocate for developing countries should also be embraced by these institutions themselves. The requisite reforms are indeed daunting, but failure to undertake the challenge will undermine any chances of an effective, multilateral system for managing globalization and development.

A second element of knowledge management for development is broad access. In addition to investing in education and research, governments can facilitate the sharing of knowledge and make special efforts to overcome the exclusion of poor communities from ideas. A particular challenge is to make knowledge available in ways and languages that can be understood by wide audiences, such as local development practitioners who do not speak English. Timely and effective information flows on issues important to poor communities can both mitigate risks and expand opportunities. Such efforts include providing market prices to poor farmers via village mobile phones, broadcasting weather information and disaster warnings on local radios, and highlighting the risks of HIV/AIDS and the benefits of public health measures in community information campaigns. In these sorts of cases, knowledge helps to empower poor people.

A third element of knowledge management for development is increased technology transfer to developing countries. Article 66.2 of the agreement on Trade-Related Aspects of Intellectual Property Rights (TRIPS) of the WTO commits developed countries to providing "incentives to enterprises and institutions in their territories for the purpose of promoting and encouraging technology transfer" to the least-developed countries. This commitment needs to be implemented in practice and applied to a wider set of countries. As outlined by Hoekman, Maskus, and Saggi (2005), this can occur through a variety of measures, including

- incentives for corporations and nongovernmental organizations to transfer mature patent rights or to provide technical assistance,
- public support for research into the specific technology needs of developing countries,
- university training for students from the low-income countries in science and technology,
- finance for participation of developing country representatives in standard-setting bodies, and
- public purchase of patents on certain technologies for free use in developing countries.

These and other steps can better ensure that knowledge in the form of international technological development is more broadly spread in the developing world.

Ideas codified into knowledge can become property when legal systems confer and enforce intellectual property rights (IPRs). The role of IPRs in economic growth and development is controversial to say the least. The standard argument is that the presence of strong intellectual property rights spurs innovation, which in turn leads to higher rates of economic growth and poverty reduction. The basis of this argument is that, if strong property rights provide good incentives for the production of things, they must also provide appropriate incentives for the production of ideas. Boldrin and Levine (2002; 2004a,b) question this assertion, arguing that intellectual property has come to mean not only the right to own and sell ideas, but also the right to regulate their use, which can create a socially inefficient monopoly. They agree that, for efficiency reasons, ideas should be protected and available for sale, just like any other commodity. They object, however, to the idea of an intellectual monopoly, arguing that monopoly is neither needed for, nor a necessary consequence of, innovation, and that intellectual property is not necessary for innovation and growth. In fact, it can hurt more than help. Boldrin and Levine suggest that, although the producers of a new product or service should have the right to benefit from its sale, they should not be able to appropriate the right of others to learn from the ideas embodied in that product. This argument has important implications for the role of ideas in globalization and development.

Since IPRs involve a key trade-off between potentially enhancing innovation and supporting the monopolization of ideas, their application requires careful analysis of both benefits and costs of conferral in order to ensure that IPR regimes promote both growth and more equitable development. How this can best be done is a question to which answers greatly diverge. We consider here the issues of patents and traditional knowledge.

Patents are a central concern with regard to the role of IPRs in development, especially in the areas of health, food, and agriculture. As summarized by Leach (2004), for instance, "The essential trade-off in choosing the patent life is that a longer patent life raises the rate at which discoveries occur, but reduces the social benefits of each discovery" (p. 175). The proponents of stronger patent protection in developing countries argue that this protection will promote domestic innovation as well as the flow of ideas through increased FDI and exports. There is not complete agreement on this matter, however. For example, Kash and Kingston (2001) argue that, in the case of complex technologies, patent protection can actually inhibit innovation. To some extent, then, the ability of increased patent protection to deliver access to knowledge and innovation is uncertain.

One suggested reform of current intellectual property arrangements is to modify rules governing patents under the TRIPS agreement to allow for patent ladders, in which the minimum extent of patent protection varies according to level of per capita income. Although designing such a system is not straightforward, this is a way to avoid what, in the case of environmental or labor standards, is disparagingly called a "one-size-fits-all" approach to the standardization of global governance systems.

One key area regarding patent protection is in the field of pharmaceuticals and the extension of patent rights to developing countries as required by TRIPS. Although some argue that the extension of intellectual property rights may lead to more research on drugs to address developing country needs, the evidence on the short experience since this extension remains hotly contested (see, for example, Lanjouw and Cockburn [2001]). There is evidence that the relatively low levels of purchasing power in developing countries and the apparent lack of commercial interest by the pharmaceutical companies remain important barriers.

Recent years have seen a number of highly significant efforts to boost investment in research and its application in developing countries. These include the Measles Initiative, the Global Alliance for Vaccines and Immunizations, the Roll Back Malaria Partnership, and the Global Fund to Fight AIDS, Tuberculosis, and Malaria. Despite these notable efforts, the recent example of the pressure placed on the governments of Brazil, India, and South Africa to honor U.S. patents on HIV/AIDS drugs, thus raising the costs of these drugs to AIDS patients in these countries, signals a remaining issue with regard to TRIPS and public health.

There appear to be two approaches to dealing with the ongoing issue of intellectual property and public health, namely the Lanjouw (2006) proposal on regional declarations in patent applications and compulsory licensing under a permanent amendment to TRIPS. Lanjouw proposes that developed-country patent systems allow for patent enforcement only in one of two regions of the world: developed countries or developing countries. In the case of what Lanjouw terms "global" diseases such as cancer or heart disease, developed-country pharmaceutical companies would choose to ensure patent protection in developed countries where markets are significantly larger, allowing for less costly delivery of generic pharmaceuticals to the developing world. In the case of "tropical" diseases such as malaria, pharmaceutical companies would choose to ensure patent protection in the developing countries, hopefully spurring innovation. Thus, the trade-off between innovation and low cost would hopefully break out in the desired fashion across global and tropical diseases.

This is an important proposal that has consequently received a good deal of attention. It may not, however, adequately cover some important diseases such as HIV/AIDS that have both global and tropical characteristics. There could indeed be cases where compulsory licensing proves to be required in order to adequately address public health crises. A 2001 Doha ministerial declaration on TRIPS and public health reconfirmed certain "flexibilities" available to protect public health, including compulsory licensing. This declaration did not, however, address the issue of the right of countries without domestic capacity to import nonpatent pharmaceuticals.[31] A 2003 WTO decision on this issue allowed poor countries to import off-patent, generic drugs under specified conditions, and directed the WTO TRIPS Council to prepare an amendment based "where appropriate" on the decision (Matthews 2004, 2006). An agreement regarding this amendment was reached in 2005 and ratified in 2007. It remains, however, both for supporting legislation in WTO member countries to be fully enacted and for the provisions of the amendment to be tested in practice.[32] It has become clear that capacity building is necessary to support use of the system.

From the point of view of poverty alleviation, it is essential that intellectual property protection be extended to traditional knowledge, folklore, and culture, or what Finger (2004) calls "poor people's knowledge." It is not only essential that intellectual property regimes allow developing countries to benefit from ideas developed in rich countries, but also that their own indigenous ideas are suitably protected. The key issue here, as expressed by Finger, is that of "enhancing the commercial value of poor people's knowledge in which there are no worries about this use being culturally offensive to members of the community or about this use undermining the traditional culture of the community" (p. 3). Unless it extends to such types of knowledge, intellectual property protection will fail to positively help poor communities. Individual country governments can help in this process by following India's lead and constructing Traditional Knowledge Digital Libraries containing formal inventories of all cultural property that its citizens might exploit in the future (Sahai 2003). This is important to prevent future theft of the country's cultural patrimony.

CONCLUSION

History and the recent experiences of many countries show that globalization can be a tool for reducing poverty. People living in poverty are less likely to remain so in a country that is exchanging its goods, services, and ideas with the rest of the world. Yet this positive impact and reach remains uneven and there is a need for global coordination and more effective global governance on issues such as armaments and climate change. Several key areas for action are outlined below.[33]

First, global trade negotiations must produce more balanced outcomes if developing countries are to be able to successfully lift their people out of poverty. Their ability to trade a wide range of goods and services must be facilitated, and rich countries must stop impeding development by the imposition of damaging tariff barriers and agricultural subsidies. For instance, there are twice as many tariff barriers imposed upon goods produced by poor people as those produced by rich countries. Nearly US$300 billion a year is spent on agricultural subsidies, which are almost worth more than the entire GDP of sub-Saharan Africa.[34] These subsidies deny developing countries export markets and damage their capability to sell their produce in their own country. These practices compound downward trends in commodity pricing, increase instability, and undermine potential for diversification into higher value-added manufactured products. Therefore, reforming the world trade system is a vital step in ensuring that all the world's inhabitants are able to reap the benefits of globalization.

The second area for action is the increased provision of aid, assistance, and debt relief to countries that demonstrate a commitment to the effective and equitable use of the additional resources. As mentioned above, aid volumes have declined during recent decades to approximately 0.25 percent of high-income countries' GDP, despite the fact that donor countries are richer now than ever before and that aid has never been more effectively used. Providing increased foreign assistance and implementing more rigorous schemes to monitor and evaluate the effective use of that aid are thus critical to ensuring that the gains provided by globalization are not reversed by bad governance and ineffective use of aid.

Foreign aid resource transfers are particularly important in the poorest countries, and much higher levels of aid are urgently required for investments in health, education, infrastructure, and for combating HIV/AIDS and other diseases. These investments cannot be financed by domestic savings alone, especially in countries that are currently crushed under burdens of debt and escaping the ravages of past corruption and mismanagement.

A third area for action is enhancing the benefits of migration and mitigating the negative effects. Remittances of over US$200 billion have flowed directly to a large number of individuals and communities (in contrast to much of aid). The transaction costs of such flows should be lowered from the current 10–15 percent to around 1 percent, which is closer to the cost of transfers between rich countries. On the other hand, the loss of highly skilled individuals in the "brain drain" needs to be mitigated, as it is a severe problem for many African and Caribbean developing countries. Addressing the problems of the current migration system and increasing its ability to provide real gains to poor people will require a multilateral as well as bilateral commitment to effective migration reform and management.

Finally, the international community should support global public goods. Three examples are in the areas of eradicating the major infectious diseases, enhancing agricultural research, and combating climate change. Most important, however, is the need for global peace and stability to prevent war and civil conflict, which do much to generate underdevelopment in many parts of the world.

Globalization has the potential to be a vehicle for shared growth, prosperity, and reductions in poverty. However, this potential is not yet being adequately realized, and the positive impacts of globalization remain uneven. Global trade equity, more and better aid, effectively benefiting from migration, and the support of global public goods are key areas for action on the route to successfully achieving development and harnessing the gains of globalization.

Notes

1. For further, more detailed discussion, we refer the reader to Goldin and Reinert (2007).
2. See, for example, James (1996, Chapter 1), O'Rourke and Williamson (1999), and World Bank (2002).
3. See Bruton (1998) for a review of import substitution industrialization.
4. See Levinson (2006) on the role of container shipping in this process.
5. See Dollar and Kraay (2004), for example. An alternative view is given in Rodríquez and Rodrik (2001). A thorough review of trade and poverty is provided by Winters, McCulloch, and McKay (2004).
6. The fact that the trade-poverty alleviation linkage is not automatic has been stressed by the United Nations Conference on Trade and Development (2004) in the case of the least developed countries.
7. Watkins and Fowler (2002) note that "In itself, trade is not inherently opposed to the interests of poor people. International trade can be a force for good, or for bad . . . The outcomes are not pre-determined. They are shaped by the way in which international trade relations are managed, and by national policies" (p. 28).
8. On the case of Bangladesh, for example, see Zohir (2001) and Watkins and Fowler (2002).
9. For a review of the evidence on trade liberalization and productivity, see Winters, McCulloch, and McKay (2004).
10. On the latter, see de Ferranti et al. (2002).
11. This point is emphasized by Reinert (2004).
12. Failure to do this weakens the claims of Rodrik and Subramanian (2008), for example.
13. The World Bank (2001) notes that "If finance is fragile, banking is the most fragile part" (p. 11).
14. For a critique of premature capital account liberalization, see Stiglitz (2000). As the World Bank (2001) notes, "Poor sequencing of financial liberalization in a poor country environment has undoubtedly contributed to bank insolvency" (p. 89). Hanson, Honohan, and Majnoni (2003) also note that "the riskiness of capital account liberalization without fiscal adjustment . . . and without reasonably strong financial regulation and supervision and a sound domestic financial system, is well recognized" (p. 10).
15. The present chapter is in broad agreement with Singh (1999), who says that "The experience of many Asian and Latin American countries with portfolio capital flows . . . indicates that the African countries would benefit from using their efforts and institutional resources to attract FDI rather than portfolio flows" (p. 356). It does, however, distinguish between portfolio flows in the form of equity investment and those in the form of bond finance, with a preference for the former.
16. Caves (1996) notes that "Survey evidence indicates that MNEs do some adapting (of technologies to labor-abundant conditions), but not a great deal, and it appears

that the costs of adaptation commonly are high relative to the benefits expected by individual companies" (p. 241).

17. Dunning (1993) notes that "With the exception of some European-based companies, the proportion of R&D activity by MNEs undertaken outside their home countries is generally quite small and, in the case of Japanese firms, negligible" (p. 301).

18. For the role of clusters in natural resource–based development, see Ramos (1998).

19. Borensztein, De Gregorio, and Lee (1998) find that it is the combination of FDI and education that has a statistically significant impact on growth.

20. Dobson and Hufbauer (2001, Chapter 1) review this evidence. Singh (1999), to some extent at least, contests this conclusion.

21. Mistakes made in these areas have proved to be too costly to the poor in the past for countries to relax their vigilance. Prasad et al. (2003) conclude that "The relative importance of different sources of financing for domestic investment, as proxied by the following three variables, has been shown to be positively associated with the incidence and the severity of currency and financial crises: the ratio of bank borrowing or other debt relative to foreign direct investment; the shortness of the term structure of external debt; and the share of external debt denominated in foreign currencies" (p. 49).

22. As emphasized by Bhinda et al. (1999), variable deposit requirements are flexible in three dimensions: 1) percentage, 2) minimum deposit period, and 3) application to new versus existing credits. These flexibilities, as well as their market-friendly nature, make variable deposit requirements an attractive policy option.

23. See, in particular, Goldin, Rogers, and Stern (2002). The overall debate on aid effectiveness is reviewed in Clemens, Radelet, and Bhavani (2004).

24. See Owens and Hoddinott (1998). As Clemens, Radelet, and Bhavani (2004) note, "This kind of assistance should have a negative simple correlation with growth, as the disaster simultaneously causes both low growth and large aid flows. While it is possible that aid might mitigate that fall in growth, any additional pathway of causation from humanitarian aid to growth is extremely difficult to detect" (p. 2).

25. In the realm of foreign aid, some (but not all) of this new thinking was reflected in World Bank (1998).

26. See Burnside and Dollar (2000). These results have been recently questioned by Easterly, Levine, and Roodman (2004).

27. The authors note that "The result is robust over a wide variety of specifications . . . It holds over various time periods, stands up whether we include or exclude influential observations, and remains robust when controlling for possible endogeneity of several independent variables" (p. 40).

28. Approaches to deal with the difficult issue of brain drain of health professionals are discussed in Martineau, Decker, and Bundred (2004).

29. This theme has been recently taken up by Sen (2006, Chapter 7), who states that "The preeminent practical challenges today include the possibility of making use of the remarkable benefits of economic connections, technological progress, and political opportunity in a way that pays adequate attention to the interests of the deprived and the underdog" (pp. 131–132).

30. As Derviş (2005) notes, "Without greater legitimacy at the supranational level, progress in solving global problems will be very difficult" (p. 3). Derviş makes very specific proposals for changing the governance structures of these institutions that deserve careful consideration.

31. This issue arises because Article 31(f) of TRIPS limits the use of pharmaceuticals produced under compulsory licenses to the *domestic* markets of producing countries.

32. Matthews (2006) notes that "It is perhaps surprising that no developing country has yet used the new mechanism to allow the importation of generic medicines following the issuance of a compulsory license in a developed country prior to patent expiry" (p. 130).

33. Further, detailed policy proposals are made in Goldin and Reinert (2007).

34. To simplify, these are roughly half in the form of producer support payments and half in the form of market price support, the latter effected through border measures. See Tokarick (2008).

References

Adams, R.H. Jr., and J. Page. 2005. "Do International Migration and Remittances Reduce Poverty in Developing Countries?" *World Development* 33(10): 1645–1669.

Adelman, I. 2001. "Fallacies in Development Theory and Their Implications for Policy." In *Frontiers of Development Economics: The Future in Perspective*, G.M. Meier and J.E. Stiglitz, eds. Oxford: Oxford University Press, pp. 103–134.

Bhattacharya, A., and S. Griffith-Jones. 2004. "The Search for a Stable and Equitable Global Financial System." In *Diversity in Development: Reconsidering the Washington Consensus*, J.J. Teunissen and A. Akkerman, eds. The Hague: Fondad, pp. 181–207.

Bhinda, N., S. Griffith-Jones, J. Leape, and M. Martin. 1999. *Private Capital Flows to Africa*. The Hague: Fondad.

Blomström, M., and A. Kokko. 2003. "Economics of Foreign Direct Investment Incentives." NBER Working Paper No. 9489. Cambridge, MA: National Bureau of Economic Research.

Blomström, M., and F. Sjöholm. 1999. "Technology Transfer and Spillovers: Does Local Participation with Multinationals Matter?" *European Economic Review* 43: 4–6, 915–923.

Boldrin, M., and D.K. Levine. 2002. "The Case against Intellectual Property." *American Economic Review* 92(2): 209–212.

———. 2004a. "The Case against Intellectual Monopoly." *International Economic Review* 45(2): 327–350.

———. 2004b. "Rent-seeking and Innovation." *Journal of Monetary Economics* 51(1): 127–160.

Boone, P. 1996. "Politics and the Effectiveness of Foreign Aid." *European Economic Review* 40(2): 289–329.

Borensztein, E., J. De Gregorio, and J.-W. Lee. 1998. "How Does Foreign Direct

Investment Affect Economic Growth?" *Journal of International Economics* 45(1): 115–135.

Bourguignon, F., and C. Morrisson. 2002. "Inequality among World Citizens: 1820–1992." *American Economic Review* 92(4): 727–744.

Bruton, H.J. 1998. "A Reconsideration of Import Substitution." *Journal of Economic Literature* 36(2): 903–936.

Burnside, C., and D. Dollar. 2000. "Aid, Policies, and Growth." *American Economic Review* 90(4): 847–868.

Caves, R.E. 1996. *Multinational Enterprise and Economic Analysis*. New York: Cambridge University Press.

Chen, S., and M. Ravallion. 2004. "How Have the World's Poorest Fared since the Early 1980s?" *World Bank Research Observer* 19(2): 141–170.

Claessens, S., D. Klingebiel, and S.L. Schmukler. 2002. "The Future of Stock Exchanges in Emerging Economies: Evolution and Prospects." *Brookings-Wharton Papers on Financial Services* 2002(1): 167–202.

Clemens, M., S. Radelet, and R. Bhavnani. 2004. "Counting Chickens When They Hatch: The Short-Term Effect of Aid on Growth." Working Paper No. 44. Washington, DC: Center for Global Development.

Collier, P., and D. Dollar. 2004. "Development Effectiveness: What Have We Learnt?" *Economic Journal* 114(496): F244–F271.

de Ferranti, D., G.E. Perry, D. Lederman, and W.F. Maloney. 2002. *From Natural Resources to the Knowledge Economy: Trade and Job Quality*. Washington, DC: World Bank.

Derviş, K. 2005. *A Better Globalization: Legitimacy, Governance, and Reform*. Washington, DC: Center for Global Development.

Dobson, W., and G.C. Hufbauer. 2001. *World Capital Markets: Challenge to the G-10*. Washington, DC: Institute for International Economics.

Dollar, D., and A. Kraay. 2004. "Trade, Growth, and Poverty." *Economic Journal* 114(493): 22–49.

Dunning, J.H. 1993. *Multinational Enterprises and the Global Economy*. Workingham, England: Addison-Wesley.

Easterly, W., R. Levine, and D. Roodman. 2004. "Aid, Policies, and Growth: Comment." *American Economic Review* 94(3): 774–780.

Eichengreen, B. 1999. *Towards a New Financial Architecture: A Practical Post-Asia Agenda*. Washington, DC: Institute for International Economics.

Finger, J.M. 2004. "Introduction and Overview." In *Poor People's Knowledge: Promoting Intellectual Property in Developing Countries*, J.M. Finger and P. Schuler, eds. Washington, DC: World Bank, pp. 1–36.

Goldin, I., and K.A. Reinert. 2007. *Globalization for Development*. Washington, DC: World Bank.

Goldin, I., H. Rogers, and N. Stern. 2002. "The Role and Effectiveness of Development Assistance: Lessons from World Bank Experience." In *A Case for Aid: Building a Consensus for Development Assistance*, James D. Wolfensohn, ed. Washington, DC: World Bank, pp. 25–183.

Hanson, J.A., P. Honohan, and G. Majnoni. 2003. "Globalization and National Financial Systems: Issues of Integration and Size." In *Globalization and National Finan-*

cial Systems, J.A. Hanson, P. Honohan, and G. Majnoni, eds. Washington, DC: World Bank, pp. 1–32.

Hatton, T.J., and J.G. Williamson. 1998. *The Age of Mass Migration: Causes and Economic Impact*. New York: Oxford University Press.

Hoekman, B.M., K.E. Maskus, and K. Saggi. 2005 "Transfer of Technology to Developing Countries: Unilateral and Multilateral Policy Options." *World Development* 33(10): 1587–1602.

James, H. 1996. *International Monetary Cooperation since Bretton Woods*. New York: Oxford University Press.

Kash, D.E., and W. Kingston. 2001. "Patents in a World of Complex Technologies." *Science and Public Policy* 28(1): 11–22.

Lanjouw, J. 2006. "A Patent Policy Proposal for Global Diseases." *Innovations* 1(1): 108–114.

Lanjouw, J.O., and I.M. Cockburn. 2001. "New Pills for Poor People? Empirical Evidence after GATT." *World Development* 29(2): 265–289.

Leach, J. 2004. *A Course in Public Economics*. Cambridge, MA: Cambridge University Press.

Levinson, M. 2006. *The Box*. Princeton, NJ: Princeton University Press.

Maddison, A. 2001. *The World Economy: A Millennial Perspective*. Paris: Organisation for Economic Co-operation and Development.

Manning, P. 2005. *Migration in World History*. New York: Routledge.

Martineau, T., K. Decker, and P. Bundred. 2004. "Brain Drain of Health Professionals: From Rhetoric to Responsible Action." *Health Policy* 70(1): 1–10.

Matthews, D. 2004. "WTO Decision on Implementation of Paragraph 6 of the Doha Declaration on the TRIPS Agreement and Public Health: A Solution to the Access to Essential Medicines Problem?" *Journal of International Economic Law* 7(1): 73–107.

———. 2006. "From the August 30, 2003 WTO Decision to the December 6, 2006 Agreement on Amendments to TRIPS: Improving Access to Medicines in Developing Countries?" *Intellectual Property Quarterly* 10(2): 91–130.

Ocampo, J.A., and J. Martin. 2003. *Globalization and Development: A Latin American and Caribbean Perspective*. Palo Alto, CA: Stanford Social Sciences.

O'Rourke, K.H., and J.G. Williamson. 1999. *Globalization and History: The Evolution of a Nineteenth-Century Atlantic Economy*. Cambridge, MA: MIT Press.

Owens, T., and J. Hoddinott. 1998. "Investing in Development or Investing in Relief: Quantifying the Poverty Tradeoffs Using Zimbabwe Household Panel Data." Working Paper Series No. WPS/99–4. Zimbabwe: Centre for the Study of African Economies.

Prasad, E., K. Rogoff, S.-J. Wei, and M.A. Kose. 2003. "Effects of Financial Globalization on Developing Countries: Some Empirical Evidence." Washington, DC: International Monetary Fund.

Ramos, J. 1998. "A Development Strategy Founded on Natural Resource-Based Production Clusters." *CEPAL Review* 66: 105–127.

Reinert, K.A. 2004. "Outcomes Assessment in Trade Policy Analysis: A Note on the Welfare Propositions of the 'Gains from Trade.'" *Journal of Economic Issues* 38(4): 1067–1073.

Reisen, H., and M. Soto. 2001. "Which Types of Capital Inflows Foster Developing-Country Growth?" *International Finance* 4(1): 1–14.

Rodrik, D., and A. Subramanian. 2008. "We Must Curb International Flows of Capital." *Financial Times.* February 25. http://www.piie.com/publications/opeds/oped.cfm?ResearchID=893 (accessed November 10, 2009).

Rodríquez, F., and D. Rodrik. 2001. "Trade Policy and Economic Growth: A Skeptic's Guide to the Cross-National Evidence." In *Macroeconomics Annual 2000.* Vol. 15, B. Bernanke and K.S. Rogoff, eds. Cambridge, MA: MIT Press, pp. 261–338.

Rousseau, P.L., and P. Wachtel. 2000. "Equity Markets and Growth: Cross-Country Evidence on Timing and Outcomes, 1980–1995." *Journal of Banking and Finance* 24(12): 1933–1957.

Sahai, S. 2003. "Indigenous Knowledge and Its Protection in India." In *Trading in Knowledge: Development Perspectives on TRIPS, Trade and Sustainability*, C. Bellmann, G. Dutfield, and R. Meléndez-Ortiz, eds. London: Earthscan, pp. 166–174.

Sen, A. 2006. *Identity and Violence: The Illusion of Destiny.* New York: Norton.

Singh, A. 1999. "Should Africa Promote Stock Market Capitalism?" *Journal of International Development* 11(3): 343–365.

Steil, B. 2001. "Creating Securities Markets in Developing Countries: A New Approach for the Age of Automated Trading." *International Finance* 4(2): 257–278.

Stiglitz, J.E. 2000. "Capital Market Liberalization, Economic Growth, and Instability." *World Development* 28(6): 1075–1086.

te Velde, D.W. 2001. *Government Policies toward Inward Foreign Direct Investment in Developing Countries.* Paris: OECD Development Center.

te Velde, D.W., and O. Morrissey. 2003. "Do Workers in Africa Get a Wage Premium If Employed in Firms Owned by Foreigners?" *Journal of African Economies* 12(1): 41–73.

Tokarick, S. 2008. "Dispelling Some Misconceptions about Agricultural Trade Liberalization." *Journal of Economic Perspectives* 22(1): 199–216.

Tsang, E.W.K., D.T. Nguyen, and M.K. Erramilli. 2004. "Knowledge Acquisition and Performance of International Joint Ventures in the Transition Economy of Vietnam." *Journal of International Marketing* 12(2): 82–103.

United Nations Conference on Trade and Development. 2004. *The Least Developed Countries Report 2004.* New York: United Nations.

Watkins, Kevin, and Penny Fowler. 2002. *Rigged Rules and Double Standards: Trade, Globalization, and the Fight Against Poverty.* Oxford: Oxfam International.

Winters, L.A., N. McCulloch, and A. McKay. 2004. "Trade Liberalization and Poverty: The Evidence So Far." *Journal of Economic Literature* 42(1): 72–115.

World Bank. 1998. *Assessing Aid: What Works, What Doesn't, and Why.* Washington, DC: World Bank.

———. 2001. *Finance for Growth: Policy Choices in a Volatile World.* Washington, DC: World Bank.

———. 2002. *Globalization, Growth, and Poverty: Building an Inclusive World Economy.* Washington, DC: World Bank.

———. 2004. *Global Development Finance: Harnessing Cyclical Gains for Development.* Washington, DC: World Bank.

Zohir, S.C. 2001. "Social Impact of the Growth of Garment Industry in Bangladesh." *Bangladesh Development Studies* 27(4): 41–80.

3
International Migration, Remittances, and Economic Development

Susan Pozo
Western Michigan University

Ask almost anyone today whether we live in a more globalized economy and you will likely hear, "Of course we do, the world is 'smaller' today than a century ago." While I agree that countries interact much more than in the past, many do not appreciate the history of that process, tending to characterize the increased globalization through trade, finance, and migration as novel. I begin this chapter by discussing economic history for a number of countries, over different time periods, and concerning different facets of globalization.

My goal is to convey three basic points concerning the world economy. The first is that globalization—sometimes referred to as economic integration—is not so new. If we look more carefully at the evidence surrounding us we find that the intermingling of people located in different corners of the globe along with their economic interactions is not unique to the present period. People and goods have crisscrossed the globe for centuries, leaving behind changes in commerce, technology, culture, and know-how.

The second point is that while the globalization process has been taking place for some time, it does in several respects manifest itself differently today. Facets of globalization and economic integration that we observe today do differ in important ways from what we observed in the past. These differences are due in part to dramatic technological advances that have taken place with respect to transportation and communication. These advances have drastically reduced prices and have expanded in many dimensions the modes that can be availed of to transport people, goods, and information.

The third point is with respect to globalization's impact on economic development. While it is often claimed that globalization disadvantages the less fortunate, causing labor dislocations and increasing income disparities around the globe, it is also the case that globalization through migration can be a powerful force with the potential to significantly improve the lot for out-migration communities in many areas of the globe (Goldberg and Pavcnik 2007). It is this facet of globalization—the spread of international migration—upon which this chapter ultimately focuses.

GLOBALIZATION IS NOT SO NEW

Countries interact with each other in a number of ways—through trade in goods and services, by borrowing and lending financial assets, and by migration. While this chapter focuses on international migration as it relates to globalization and economic development, it begins with a detour into more familiar and established territory for most readers. I first present data on globalization as measured by the share of international trade in GDP—an openness index. This particular index or one of its close variants is what researchers usually cite when making the case that the world is much more integrated today, that economies today interact substantially more with each other relative to the past.

The notion that globalization is of recent vintage probably originates from the analysis of an openness index relative to its value 50 or 60 years ago. For example, take the case of the United States. Figure 3.1 shows the ratio of U.S. international trade flows (U.S. exports plus U.S. imports) to U.S. national income (GDP) since 1945. The graph clearly suggests that international trade (as a share of GDP) was relatively level to 1970 and then consistently grew. Diagrams such as the one plotted in Figure 3.1 are the basis of the general perception that the U.S. economy was fairly closed economically with respect to the rest of the world until fairly recently.

By contrast, an examination of Figure 3.2, where this same series is plotted from 1870 to the present, provides us with an entirely different impression. What emerges from this broader timeline of U.S. economic history is that today's relatively high fraction of trade in U.S. GDP is

Figure 3.1 Trade as a Share of GDP in the United States, 1945–2001

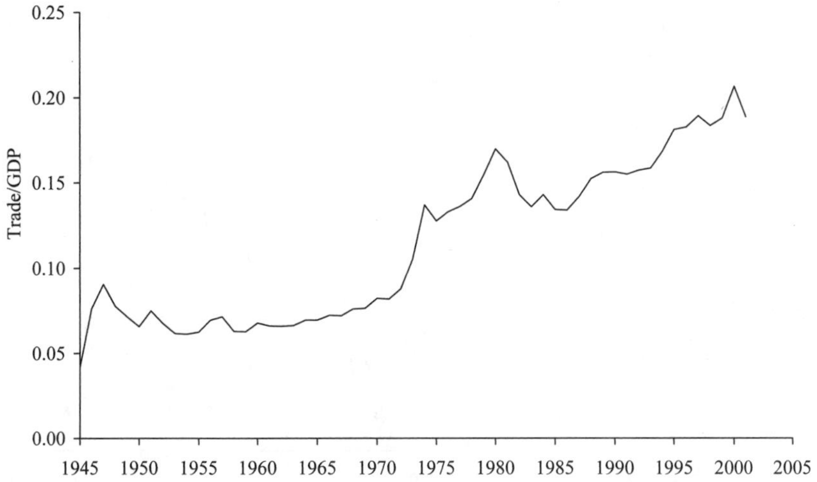

SOURCE: Author's calculations from Carter et al. (2006, Series Ee419, Ee422, Ca10).

neither unique nor new. In 1916 merchandise trade as a share of GDP was 19.7 percent, exceeding the 18.9 percent share observed in 2001. The plot suggests that the argument that globalization is new is generally derived from an examination of data since World War II. But if we instead peer further back, a totally different picture emerges. We observe relatively low trade flows during and surrounding the interwar period (World War I through World War II). The interwar period and period immediately surrounding it with its relatively low share of trade in GDP appear as an exception to the rule. Both before and after that period, international trade played larger roles in the U.S. economy.

It is understandable that researchers tend to analyze economic flows since World War II, generally disregarding or shying away from economic data series prior to the interwar period. Since World War II, governments and international organizations have become more interested in collecting economic data in a systematic and consistent manner.[1] International organizations such as the United Nations, the World Bank, the OECD, and the International Monetary Fund have expended considerable effort and resources to facilitate and coordinate the collection of data so that economic information is readily available and compa-

Figure 3.2 Trade as a Share of GDP, United States

SOURCE: Author's calculations from Carter et al. (2006, Series Ee416, Ee417, Ee419, Ee422, Ca10).

rable across countries and over time.[2] Consequently, series since World War II have become more reliable, tempting researchers to restrict their research to the analysis of recent data, or at a minimum, the post–World War II period. There are drawbacks, however, to limiting our analysis to more recent data. We fail to appreciate important changes and turning points in the time series of flows, compromising our understanding of economic activity both in the short and long run.

Yet another picture emerges of globalization through trade if we examine a century of data for Argentina. Figure 3.3 displays an index of openness obtained by expressing the sum of Argentina's exports and imports as a share of GDP. While total merchandise trade was equal to about half of Argentina's GDP at the turn of the last century (i.e., in 1900), Argentina's trade accounted for less than one-fifth of GDP in 2000. Using simple indexes of openness, Argentina appears less globalized today relative to yesterday. In the Southern Cone, globalization through international trade has faltered rather than grown.

Misconceptions regarding the globalization of economies through migration also arise if we similarly limit ourselves to analyzing recent

Figure 3.3 Trade as a Share of GDP, Argentina

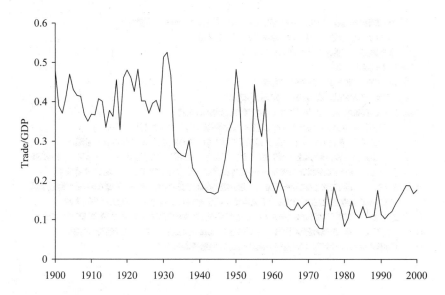

SOURCE: Computed from Astorga et al. (2002).

data on migration. U.S. data on the percentage of the U.S. population that is foreign born is presented in Figure 3.4. These data are from the U.S. decennial census. If we restrict the analysis to data from the 1970s to the present we observe that the U.S. population has become increasingly foreign born, from about 5 percent to 12 percent of the U.S. population. However, a longer-run view reveals that during the late 1800s and early 1900s, an even greater percentage of the U.S. population was foreign born, hovering at 15 percent.

Economic history provides us with many examples of globalization from earlier time periods that parallel the process we see occurring today. For example, Molina (2008) suggests that legal changes with respect to China, both in 1882 and in 2001, in turn impacted Mexican-U.S. migratory flows in substantial ways. The Chinese Exclusion Act of 1882, which effectively shut down Chinese immigration to the United States, was followed by a substantial rise in Mexican immigrants to the United States, presumably due to labor shortages caused by the exclusion of Chinese labor. One hundred twenty years later, the acceptance

Figure 3.4 Percentage of U.S. Population That Is Foreign Born

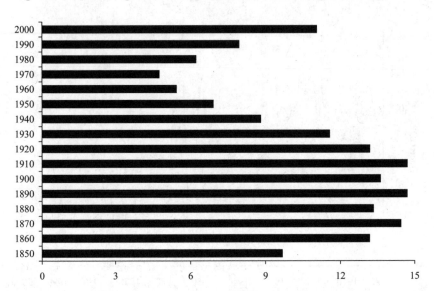

SOURCE: Author's calculations from Carter et al. (2006, Series Ad354, Aa2).

of China into the World Trade Organization seems to have had a similar impact, that of stimulating Mexican-U.S. immigration. With China a formal member of the world trading system, the relative competitiveness of Mexican industry seems to have been reduced, causing an excess supply of Mexican labor. The excess supply seems to have found an outlet in the U.S. labor market, which proved relatively eager to absorb that Mexican labor. Hence both in 1882 and in 2001, changes in immigration statutes with respect to Chinese nationals have impacted Mexico-U.S. economic flows. The interactions across countries that we observe today and are attributed to "globalization" are similarly found in yesterday's world.

Another example of economic integration both in the past and today is with respect to workers' remittances. As of late, the popular press has consistently reported on the large flows of immigrants' earnings that are sent to their home communities (DeParle 2007, 2008). The main point in these articles is that these flows of money have not been adequately recognized in the past, in part because they were relatively small and have only recently been of much significance. But the notion that remittances were not important or significant in earlier time periods is not corroborated by the historical data I have collected on Italian remittances. Figure 3.5 shows the ratio of remittances sent by Italian emigrants relative to Italian GNP in order to measure the relative size of the flows over time.[3] The figure shows averages of this ratio for each decade from the 1860s through the 1930s. Around the turn of the century, cross-border money flows from Italian-origin immigrants to their families remaining in Italy accounted for about 4 or 5 percent of Italian national income. The remarkable aspect of this value is that remittances to Mexico are currently considered to be at their highest, but not even reaching 3 percent of Mexico's national income.[4] Hence, in relation to national income, remittances were more important to Italy in 1900 than they are to Mexico today, even though the levels of remittances to Mexico now are considered to be extraordinarily large and newsworthy.

Figure 3.5 Remittance Receipts as a Percentage of GNP: Italy 1860–1930

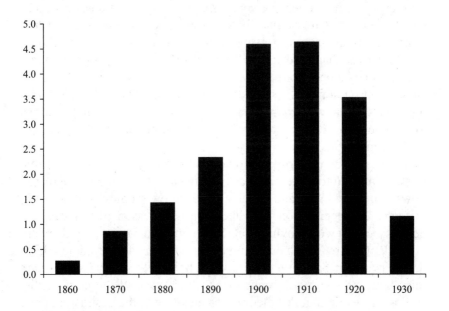

SOURCE: Author's calculations from information contained in Mitchell (1998) and Cinel (1991).

GLOBALIZATION MANIFESTS ITSELF DIFFERENTLY TODAY RELATIVE TO YESTERDAY

There is considerable evidence that the interchange of goods, the migrations of people, and the international flows of financial assets have a long economic history. The case can be made, however, that today's interactions differ in important respects from the interactions of economies yesterday. Technological advances have changed the nature of international trade and the context in which immigration, emigration, and international money flows take place. This section discusses how two economic sectors—transportation and communication—have affected the globalization process.

While commentaries today tend to suggest that the observed increased trade globalization is a result of changes in the willingness of countries to open up to foreign markets (such as through the formation of global, regional, and bilateral trade liberalization pacts), economic historians are placing more weight on technological change as the main driving force. It has become substantially cheaper to transport goods, people, and ideas today than it was a century ago, and these reductions in costs are generally attributed to technological advances. Figure 3.6 displays Mohammed and Williamson's (2004) calculations of a real global tramp shipping price index, showing that shipping rates in 1994 were about one-third of 1870 rates in real terms. These reduced transportation costs have certainly played a role in allowing trading patterns to become more complex, to involve more nations, and to change direction at a moment's notice.

While declining transportation costs have played an important role in stimulating trade, they also are responsible for inducing increased flows of people, ideas, and financial assets. Lower transportation costs, of course, make migration more likely due to the easing of financial burdens associated with moving from one country to another, but there are other channels by which declining transportation costs promote migration. Lower transportation costs ease the pain and risks that accompany migration, inducing more migration to take place. If the migrant discovers that work is not as plentiful or lucrative in the destination area, lower fares will permit the return of the migrant to her point of origin or to another destination. The reversibility of migration is likely to induce

Figure 3.6 Real Global Transportation Cost Index: 1870–1994

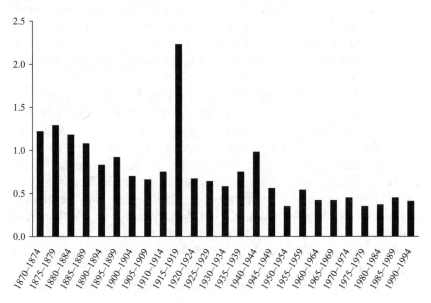

SOURCE: Data from Mohammed and Williamson (2004, Table 3).

a greater volume of flows and a more diverse set of migrants. Temporary immigrants are likely to be more plentiful, and migrants can afford to travel farther away. Cheaper fares also promote tourism and the ability to learn about other unfamiliar regions of the world, facilitating subsequent migration. But most importantly for our focus, reduced transportation costs encourage continued interactions of migrants with their home communities, which is important for economic development—a point I argue in the next section.

While reductions in transportation costs have significantly facilitated the transport of goods and people, reductions in communication costs have been even more substantial and have likely resulted in even greater changes in global economic relations. Table 3.1 displays telephone rates for New York to London and New York to Buenos Aires (for a three-minute call) from the inception of telephone service in that market to 1981. The first two columns report nominal telephone rates, while the third and fourth columns express those same rates in real terms.[5] The inflation-indexed series indicates that transatlantic calls were 130 times more expensive in 1927 relative to calls made in 1981. While the 1927 rate appears to be fantastically high, one must recall the capital stock that went into providing one telephone conversation at that time. For example, when telephone service was initiated from New York to San Francisco in 1915, the system could accommodate only one conversation at a time (Field 2006).

The ease with which migrants can now keep in touch with individuals living far away has substantially changed the relations that migrants have with the family members that did not accompany them. Migrants' ties with the home community are stronger and longer-lasting, with better information flows in both directions. Migrants can remain abreast of the continuing or the sporadic needs of the family back home. News of sickness, marriages, or business opportunities can now be quickly and relatively cheaply communicated. Money transfers, whether from migrant to family or family to migrant, are easily tracked and made more secure by the ability of the sender to pair the money transfer with a telephone call to the recipient.[6] And regardless of the migrant's or the family's ability to read and write, communication is easy and readily accessible.

In their study of international trade, Freund and Weinhold (2004) find that the Internet has increased the rate of growth of exports. It is logical to also presume that the Internet has changed the nature of human migration. It has vastly increased the ability of individuals, with or without migration networks, to secure pertinent information prior to migration. By obtaining such information, migrants increase the odds of having a successful migration. The Internet has also vastly reduced the costs of keeping in contact with family and friends left behind. This is likely to ease the pain of separation, further inducing migratory flows.

In sum, lower transportation costs and communications costs due to technological advances have had significant impacts on the environment in which international migration takes place. Lower transportation costs allow, of course, for a greater volume of overall migration, but also for more return migration. More temporary or short-term migration is also encouraged since migrants require smaller rewards in order to recover the costs of moving from one region of the world to another. Advances in communications technology keep migrants informed of home events, of the everyday or acute needs of the family, strengthening family and community migration networks, even among the illiterate.

Table 3.1 Nominal and Real Telephone Rates from the Beginning of Telephone Service to 1981

Year	Nominal prices for a 3-minute call from NY to:		Real prices for a 3-minute call from NY to:	
	London	Buenos Aires	London	Buenos Aires
1927	75.0	—	793.1	—
1928	45.0	—	484.2	—
1929	45.0	—	484.2	—
1930	30.0	36.0	330.5	396.6
1931	30.0	30.0	363.1	363.1
1932	30.0	30.0	402.9	402.9
1934	30.0	30.0	411.9	411.9
1936	21.0	21.0	277.9	277.9
1937	21.0	21.0	268.3	268.3
1939	21.0	15.0	277.9	198.5
1940	21.0	15.0	276.0	197.1
1941	21.0	15.0	262.8	187.7
1944	21.0	12.0	219.5	125.4
1945	12.0	12.0	122.6	122.6
1946	12.0	12.0	113.2	113.2
1952	12.0	12.0	83.3	83.3
1959	12.0	12.0	75.8	75.8
1960	12.0	12.0	74.5	74.5
1965	12.0	12.0	70.0	70.0
1967	12.0	12.0	66.1	66.1
1968	12.0	12.0	63.4	63.4
1970	9.6	12.0	45.5	56.9
1972	9.6	12.0	42.2	52.8
1973	9.6	12.0	39.7	49.7
1974	3.6	8.0	13.4	29.8
1975	3.6	8.0	12.3	27.3
1976	3.6	8.0	11.6	25.8
1977	3.6	8.0	10.9	24.2
1978	4.5	8.0	12.6	22.5
1980	4.8	7.0	10.7	15.7
1981	3.0	4.5	6.0	9.1

NOTE: Real prices are expressed in 2003 dollars. See note 5 for details.
SOURCE: Nominal telephone rates are from Carter et al. (2006). Real telephone rates are computed by the author applying a consumer price index from the same source.

GLOBALIZATION AND ECONOMIC DEVELOPMENT

This section discusses a sampling of the channels by which migration and its by-products impact economic development. These channels have been fortified by the dramatic decreases in transportation costs that we have observed and by the improvements in communications technologies that continue to this date. These have greatly facilitated migration and the continued interactions between migrants living afar and the family back home. I begin with a discussion of migration's impact on economic growth in origin communities and follow with how emigrants' by-products affect growth and development back home.

Cheaper transportation and better communications across countries help to lower barriers to migration and therefore have the potential to greatly expand the level of temporary international migration that takes place. Take, for example, the nearly threefold increase in foreign student enrollments in the United States (from 1.4 percent of all U.S. students for the 1954–1955 academic year to 3.9 percent of U.S. higher education enrollment during the 2006–2007 academic year [Institute of International Education 2006]). Undoubtedly, lower transportation costs and the ease with which parents and students can communicate despite great distances has aided in that growth. Reductions in nonpecuniary and monetary costs must improve the cost-benefit ratio, encouraging foreign study, the subsequent return home, and the eventual transmission, to poor countries, of technical and scientific expertise by students originating from those countries.

The contribution toward economic development that students can make when they study abroad is not limited to the human capital that they repatriate home at the conclusion of their sojourn at universities abroad. Networks are created between these students and their professors, between international and domestic students, and between international students from one country and international students from other countries. In today's world, these networks are likely to prove stronger and longer lasting given the variety of ways by which we cheaply communicate to most areas of the world. Foreign study by students, therefore, results in the flow of knowledge and expertise to poor countries. This continued flow is especially possible today given the advent of nearly costless forms of communication such as e-mail and Voice over Internet Protocol.

At this juncture it is appropriate to ask whether poor countries also pay a price for the facilitated flow of students across countries. While it may be easier for students to flow from poor countries to rich countries to acquire education, the flow also can go in the other direction. Individuals who have already received training or education in poor countries emigrate to richer countries with hopes of higher wages and expanded opportunities. This results in "brain drain," weakening the prospects for development in poorer regions of the world as these nations lose scarce human capital. This concern is of paramount importance given that, as of late, developed countries have modified their immigration policies to favor skilled immigration over family reunification immigration, stimulating the exodus of educated individuals from all areas of the globe. Given the expected income differentials to migration, the highly educated from poorer regions of the world are particularly motivated. The origin communities are not only deprived of talented individuals, they are also put into the position of subsidizing human capital acquisition that ultimately benefits rich nations, since in many cases the education is acquired at the developing country's expense. For example, one estimate for 2004 suggests that 26 percent of Somali-trained physicians practice abroad. During that same year there were 4 physicians per 100,000 persons in Somalia, a far cry from the U.S. ratio of 300 physicians per 100,000 population (Docquier and Bhargava 2006). The possibility that easier emigration can strip poor countries of scarce resources that are important for development is a real concern.

On the flip side of the brain drain debate is the argument that the emigration of the highly educated leads to "brain gain." If there is the possibility of out-migration of the more highly educated (because of the possibility of accruing higher returns for one's talents and expertise abroad), there will be greater competition for the "emigration slots," leading to increases in overall investments in human capital accumulation as individuals attempt to distinguish themselves from others vying for visas. Stark, Helmenstein, and Prskawetz (1997) argue that the resulting brain gain exceeds the brain loss. Others, including Schiff (2006), disagree that the gains are greater than the losses and see the emigration of the highly skilled as generally disadvantaging the labor-exporting nations.

Individuals who emigrate on a temporary basis can also bring home expertise acquired in ways other than through formal education. For example, McCormick and Wahba (2001) find that temporary emigrants who have worked abroad in previously unfamiliar labor markets return home not only with capital to begin new businesses, but also with entrepreneurial abilities from that experience. By observing other forms of "doing business" and other uses of technology, emigrants learn how to become more flexible and to take advantage of opportunities that may await them in the communities to which they return.

Foreign direct investment has also vastly expanded in today's world, and it is often credited with promoting economic development in capital-poor countries. But the acquisition of *physical* capital isn't the only channel by which growth is stimulated when FDI takes place. Top-level managers, scientists, and engineers from the home office often accompany FDI. In the process of putting in place the physical capital— manufacturing the goods for sale and delivering the firm's services— the home office employees tend to transfer technology and know-how from countries that tend to be well-endowed with these resources to more poorly endowed areas.

Social remittances, "a local-level, migration-driven form of cultural diffusion," is yet another avenue by which migration may influence economic development (Levitt 1998). Return migrants resettling back home share ideas, technology, expectations, and familiarity with foreign institutions and foreign markets, which in turn can facilitate economic development. Those who visit home temporarily and communicate often with their families may also be helping to lift their home countries from poverty.[7]

Emigration has also been found to stimulate trade in goods and services between pairs of labor exporting and labor importing nations (Mundra 2005). This type of international trade is sometimes referred to as "nostalgic trade." Mexican immigrants in the United States yearning for traditional foods and beverages demand these in the U.S. marketplace, stimulating merchandise trade and promoting agricultural production back home. After a while, these products can become known and favored by the host country population and stimulate that trade on a broader basis, as in the case of the popularity of Mexican cuisine in the United States today.

An extremely important by-product of migration is the flow of money that immigrants send home. These are referred to as workers' remittances and have gained the interest of bankers, academicians, and government policymakers. On a number of levels these flows have been credited with stimulating economic development.

Earlier we established that temporary migration is likely to be stimulated by the dramatic decreases that have taken place with respect to transportation costs. Likewise, by easing the continuation of contacts among families separated by long distances, reductions in communications costs make migration for the purpose of earning money abroad much more palatable. In short, increases in temporary migration to earn wages in a geographically distant land increase the flow of remittances across borders. In addition, given that money transfers today are less costly and more secure, it is more likely that resources flow back home on a periodic basis. The receipt of remittances can contribute toward economic development by compensating for liquidity constraints often encountered in poorer regions of the world. Remittances have been linked to investments in existing businesses in the Dominican Republic as measured by Amuedo-Dorantes and Pozo (2006), while Woodruff and Zenteno (2007) find that the existence of migration networks (which they presume signals greater access to remittance receipts) appears to increase profits and capital investment in Mexican microenterprises located in urban areas. Remittances have also been linked to increases in educational investments in a number of studies, including studies using Haitian, Dominican, and El Salvadorian data. (See Amuedo-Dorantes, Georges, and Pozo [forthcoming]; Amuedo-Dorantes and Pozo [2009]; and Edwards and Ureta [2003], respectively.)

Remittances have also been credited with reducing the incidence of "sudden stops" of capital inflows (Bugamelli and Paterno 2005). Countries that experience large inflows of remittances are thought to be less vulnerable to economic recessions and global crises given the belief that substantial levels of these flows are motivated by altruism. Altruistic inflows will tend to be countercyclical, reducing the damage that foreign investors may impart when they become concerned with a poorly performing economy and withdraw resources. The countercyclical nature of the flows from the emigrants who remit are likely to be stronger if they are better informed about the immediate situation and the economic needs of their families back home. If the emigrants know that times are bad for their families, they will remit more. And as they learn that economic recovery is on the way, they are likely to remit less. It is logical to assume that cheaper and better communications have led to improvements in the timing of altruistic remittance inflows so that they can better serve in this countercyclical manner. Consequently, it is plausible that remittances reduce the threat of currency crises. Foreign investors are less likely to behave in ways that destabilize the currency in the face of this vast force of remitters who will naturally provide resources to the family back home as unfavorable shocks hit the economy.

Remittances have also been found to encourage the development of infrastructures that facilitate development. Demirgüc-Kunt et al. (2009) purport to find that the channelling of substantial sums of money by emigrants to their families in Mexico has provided incentives for financial intermediaries to locate in the migrant sending areas. Financial intermediaries are in effect taking advantage of increased demand for services that result from the money inflows that emigrants send home. This is especially important in the case of Mexico, given that there has traditionally been relatively more out-migration in Mexico's rural and less-developed areas of the country—the same areas that traditionally have been ignored by the banking system.

DISCUSSION AND CONCLUSIONS

Globalization has been progressing for some time, rising and falling, but it is certainly not unique to our times. The perception that growth in these economic interactions is of only recent vintage might originate from limiting ourselves to examining data from the latter half of the twentieth century, where these patterns are not obvious, driving us to conclude that globalization is a product of the past 50 or so years. In contrast, once we examine data from earlier time periods, we find that globalization through trade, finance, and migration has a much longer history.

While the globalization process was certainly born before the past half century, there appear to be differences in the interactions of countries today relative to yesterday that are worth dwelling on. This chapter focuses on international migration in particular, pointing to the context in which migration took place in the past relative to today. Technological advances have translated into widespread reductions in transportation and international communications costs. Migrants, potential migrants, and the families living back home all have access to much better information, reducing the risks involved with migration and increasing the flow of information between families living in different parts of the world. This has the potential to greatly improve the lives of migrants, their families, and the communities from which migrants originate.

Lower transportation and communications costs today keep emigrants abreast of events back home. Emigrants and the families from which they originate can easily and cheaply maintain ties with one another. Migrants know what is happening back home and what the needs of the family may be on a day-to-day basis. The families that remain in the home community have clearer perceptions of the lives and activities of their family abroad. In earlier time periods, these communications were less accessible and likely caused greater numbers of migrants to lose touch with their families back home, leading to lower flows of resources back home and fewer instances of the return of information that could be used to stimulate economic development.

It is interesting that there have been substantial calls for globalization in some dimensions and calls for restrictions in others. While arguments are made in favor of unimpeded flows of capital and of goods across countries, the same cannot be said about people flows. Economists often lobby for the free flow of capital from areas where capital is abundant and earning lower returns to areas where capital is scarce and earning higher returns, but we do not as often and as vigorously argue that labor should move from areas where its return is lower to areas where its return is higher. While we tend to claim that international trade in goods and services is not a zero-sum game, but rather benefits both importing and exporting nations in the aggregate, we do not as consistently attribute likewise to the migrations of people.

Despite the impediments to migration that we tend to observe, technological changes that have swept the transportation and communications sectors are likely to continue, propelling growth in migratory flows and their by-products. It is up to us to make the most of the potential gains from the movement of resources to areas where they reap the greatest gain, helping to free communities from poverty.

Notes

1. For a discussion of the comparability of pre- and postwar data for the United States, see Romer (1986).
2. For example, see Lemaitre (2005) for a discussion of the harmonization of migration statistics across countries and Alexander, Cady, and Gonzalez-Garcia (2008) for discussion of the IMF's extensive program on data standards, harmonization, and dissemination.
3. I obtained nominal inflows of remittances to Italy from Cinel's (1991) historical account of Italian emigration, its impacts and by-products over the 1860 through 1930 period. Cinel does not provide remittance amounts for each year. Data on Italian GNP were obtained from Mitchell (1998). I computed a remittance to GNP value for each decade using the data that were available within each decade.
4. The Mexican Central Bank reports that remittances to Mexico were US$23,969.5 million in 2007 while its GDP stood at US$893,364 million. Remittances therefore accounted for only 2.68 percent of Mexico's national income.
5. Nominal telephone rates (for a three-minute call) are from Historical Statistics of the United States, series Dg60 and Dg63. Real telephone rates are computed by the author applying consumer price index series Cc1 from the same source. Given the base of the series, the rates are therefore expressed in 2003 dollars.
6. In some markets, Western Union's money transfer fee includes a three-minute telephone call from the sender of money to the money recipient. The call can be used, for example, to advise the recipient of the transfer, the amount being transferred, and how to retrieve it.
7. Social remittance can also transfer undesirable habits and culture that can have detrimental impacts on growth and development, as in the case of the rise of gang violence thought to be imported to Central America from Los Angeles. See Archibold (2007).

References

Alexander, William E., John Cady, and Jesus Gonzalez-Garcia. 2008. *The IMF's Data Dissemination Initiative after 10 Years*. Washington, DC: International Monetary Fund.

Amuedo-Dorantes, Catalina, Annie Georges, and Susan Pozo. Forthcoming. "Migration, Remittances, and Children's Schooling in Haiti." *The Annals of the American Academy of Political and Social Science.*

Amuedo-Dorantes, Catalina, and Susan Pozo. 2006. "Remittance Receipt and Business Ownership in the Dominican Republic." *World Economy* 29(7): 939–956.

———. 2009. "Accounting for Remittance Migration: Effects on Children's Schooling." Unpublished manuscript. Western Michigan University, Kalamazoo, MI.

Archibold, Ronald C. 2007. "Officials See a Spread in Activity of Gangs." *New York Times*, February 8, A:14.

Astorga, P., A. Bergés, E.V.K. Fitzgerald, and R. Thorp. 2002. *Oxford Latin American Economic History Database.* Oxford: Oxford University. http://oxlad.qeh.ox.ac.uk/ (accessed November 23, 2009).

Bugamelli, Matteo, and Francesco Paterno. 2005. "Do Workers' Remittances Reduce the Probability of Current Account Reversals?" Policy Research Working Paper Series 3766. Washington, DC: World Bank.

Carter, Susan B., Scott Sigmund Gartner, Michael R. Haines, Alan L. Olmstead, Richard Sutch, and Gavin Wright, eds. 2006. *Historical Statistics of the United States, Earliest Times to the Present: Millennial Edition.* New York: Cambridge University Press.

Cinel, Dino. 1991. *The National Integration of Italian Return Migration, 1870–1929.* Cambridge: Cambridge University Press.

Demirgüc-Kunt, Asli, Ernesto López Córdova, María Soledad Martínez Pería, and Christopher Woodruff. 2009. "Remittances and Banking Services: Evidence from Mexico." World Bank Policy Research Working Paper No. 4983. Washington, DC: World Bank.

DeParle, Jason. 2007. "Migrant Money Flow: A $300 Billion Current." *New York Times*, November 18, WK:3.

———. 2008. "World Banker and His Cash Return Home." *New York Times*, March 17, A:1.

Docquier, Frederic, and Alok Bhargava. 2006. "Medical Brain Drain: Physicians' Emigration Rates, 1991–2004." Washington, DC: World Bank. http://go.worldbankorg/9Y0NKDQK60 (accessed November 23, 2009).

Edwards, Alejandra Cox, and Manuelita Ureta. 2003. "International Migration, Remittances, and Schooling: Evidence from El Salvador." *Journal of Development Economics*, Special Issue (72)2: 429–461.

Field, Alexander J. 2006. "Communications." In *Historical Statistics of the United States: Millennial Edition,* Vol. 4. Susan B. Carter, Scott Sigmund Gartner, Michael R. Haines, Alan L. Olmstead, Richard Sutch, and Gavin Wright, eds. New York: Cambridge University Press, pp. 4-997–4-1059.

Freund, Caroline L., and Diana Weinhold. 2004. "The Effect of the Internet on International Trade." *Journal of International Economics* 62(1): 171–189.

Goldberg, Pinelopi Koujianou, and Nina Pavcnik. 2007. "Distributional Effects of Globalization in Developing Countries." *Journal of Economic Literature* 45(1): 39–82.

Institute of International Education. 2006. "Open Doors 2006 Fast Facts." New York: Institute of International Education. http://opendoors.iienetwork.org/?p=113122 (accessed August 18, 2009).

Lemaitre, Georges. 2005. "The Comparability of International Migration

Statistics: Problems and Prospects." OECD Statistics Brief No. 9. Paris: OECD.

Levitt, Peggy. 1998. "Social Remittances: Migration Driven Local-Level Forms of Cultural Diffusion." *International Migration Review* 42(4): 926–948.

McCormick, Barry, and Jackline Wahba. 2001. "Overseas Work Experience, Savings and Entrepreneurship amongst Return Migrants to LDCs." *Scottish Journal of Political Economy* 48(2): 164–178.

Mitchell, B.R. 1998. *International Historical Statistics, Europe 1750–1993.* New York: Stockton Press.

Mohammed, S.I.S., and J.G. Williamson. 2004. "Freight Rates and Productivity Gains in British Tramp Shipping 1869–1950." *Explorations in Economic History* 41(2): 172–203.

Molina, David J. 2008. "The Recycling Centenarian Trio: U.S., Mexico, China." Unpublished manuscript. University of North Texas, Denton, TX.

Mundra, Kusum. 2005. "Immigration and International Trade: A Semiparametric Empirical Investigation." *Journal of International Trade and Economic Development* 14(1): 65–91.

Romer, Christina D. 1986. "Is the Stabilization of the Postwar Economy a Figment of the Data?" *American Economic Review* 76(3): 314–334.

Schiff, Maurice. 2006. "Brain Gain: Claims about Its Size and Impact Are Greatly Exaggerated." In *International Migration, Remittances, and the Brain Drain*, Çağlar Ozden and Maurice Schiff, eds. Washington, DC: World Bank.

Stark, Oded, Christian Helmenstein, and Alexia Prskawetz. 1997. "A Brain Gain with a Brain Drain." *Economics Letters* 55(2): 227–234.

Woodruff, Christopher, and Rene Zenteno. 2007. "Migration Networks and Microenterprises in Mexico." *Journal of Development Economics* 82(2): 509–528.

4

Globalization and Inequality among Nations

Joseph P. Joyce
Wellesley College

In 1870, at the beginning of the first modern era of globalization, the world's average per capita GDP was $873 (see Table 4.1).[1] Average income in the richest nations—the United States, Canada, Australia, and New Zealand—was $2,419, while income in the poorest—the African nations—was $500, a spread of 5:1. By 1950, at the start of the second era of globalization, income had risen to $9,268 in the same upper-income group, but only $890 in the African nations, and the spread had risen to 13:1. By 2003, the corresponding income levels were $28,039 and $1,549, and the spread between the top and the bottom of the international distribution of income stood at 18:1.

These aggregate figures masked even greater disparities among countries. In 2006, the Democratic Republic of the Congo, a country with a population of approximately 57 million people, had a GDP per capita of $649. That same year, France, with a population of 60 million, recorded per capita income of $28,877.[2] The ratio of the income of the average French citizen to a citizen of the African country was over 40:1.

The disparity in global income has become the focus of much scrutiny, inquiry, and debate. The questions that have arisen include: What are the causes of these disparities? Is inequality among nations a consequence of globalization? How should the upper-income countries respond?

Among those who have sought to answer these questions have been a number of noted philosophers, including Rawls (1999), Pogge (2002, 2005), Risse (2005a,b,c) and Nussbaum (2006). Rawls, for example, in *The Law of Peoples* (1999), writes: " . . . the causes of the wealth of a people and the forms it takes lie in their political culture and in the religious, philosophical, and moral traditions that support the basic

Table 4.1 Per Capita GDP (1990 international dollars)

	1870	1913	1950	1973	2003
Western Europe	1,960	3,457	4,578	11,417	19,912
U.S., Canada, Australia, NZ	2,419	5,233	9,268	16,179	28,039
Asia	556	696	717	1,718	4,434
Latin America	676	1,494	2,503	4,513	5,786
Eastern Europe & USSR	941	1,558	2,602	5,731	5,705
Africa	500	637	890	1,410	1,549
World	873	1,526	2,113	4,091	6,516
Spread	4.8	8.2	13.0	11.5	18.1

SOURCE: Maddison (2007).

structure of their political and social institutions, as well as in the indus-triousness and cooperative talents of its members, all supported by their political virtues" (p. 108).

The "burdened societies" lack the ability to function at a level of economic activity which allows their citizens to secure the minimum levels of subsistence, shelter, health care, etc. Rawls (1999) contends that the "well-ordered" societies have a duty to assist these burdened nations. However, the duty is not a distributive one; rather, the goal of assistance is to help these nations manage their own affairs.

Nussbaum (2006) criticizes Rawls for his assumption that states have equal standing in the global economy. She writes that to " . . . assume a rough equality between parties is to assume something so grossly false of the world as to make the resulting theory unable to address the world's most urgent problems . . ." (p. 235). She states that we need to " . . . acknowledge the fact that the international economic system, and the activities of multinational corporations, creates severe, dispropor-tionate burdens for poorer nations, which cannot solve their problems by wise internal policies alone" (p. 240).

Economic analysis cannot evaluate the philosophical merits of these different responses, but it can shed some light on the reasons for the dis-parity across nations in income levels and the role of globalization in their propagation. A better understanding of the reasons for economic inequality can yield insights into the reasons why some nations prosper over time but others do not, and what could be done about this disparity.

This chapter reviews several studies that have sought to clarify these issues.

The next section of this chapter offers a survey of the different explanations that have been offered to explain the disparity in global income and the results of empirical analyses that have sought to distinguish among them. The third section summarizes the research on the development of institutions, and the fourth section addresses the issue of how globalization affects the poor. The last section offers some suggestions for how globalization can be managed to provide more opportunities for the poorest nations.

SOURCES OF INEQUALITY

Inequality has long been a characteristic of the world economy. The differences in the levels of income per capita reflect variations in the growth of income in different regions, and these rates have also varied over time (see Table 4.2). The growth of per capita GDP in Western Europe, for example, rose to 1.33 percent during the first era of globalization, 1870–1913, and then fell to 0.76 percent during the time of the two world wars and the intervening period. But it rose fivefold to 4.05 percent when globalization regained its momentum after 1950, before falling to 1.87 percent after 1973. Growth per capita in Asia rose from

Table 4.2 Growth Rates of Per Capita GDP (%)

	1820–1870	1870–1913	1913–1950	1950–1973	1973–2003
Western Europe	0.98	1.33	0.76	4.05	1.87
U.S., Canada, Australia, NZ	1.41	1.81	1.56	2.45	1.85
Asia	−0.09	0.52	0.08	3.87	3.21
Latin America	−0.03	1.86	1.40	2.60	0.83
Eastern Europe & USSR	0.63	1.18	1.40	3.49	−0.02
Africa	0.35	0.57	0.91	2.02	0.32
World	0.54	1.30	0.88	2.91	1.56

SOURCE: Maddison (2007).

0.08 percent during the wartime period to 3.87 percent from 1950 to 1973 and 3.21 percent in the more recent era. Between 1950 and 2003, Asia's share of world GDP more than doubled, from 18.6 percent to 40.5 percent (see Table 4.3).

The sources of economic growth have become the subject of much theoretical and empirical analysis in recent decades.[3] Economists have sought to look beyond the short-term fluctuations of the business cycle to identify the determinants of a country's productive capacity. Barro (1997), in a summary of the work that he and others have done on this topic, includes the initial level of per capita income, school enrollment rates, and changes in the terms of trade among the determinants of the growth of real per capita income. Theoretical studies have focused on the role of technological innovation in sustaining growth over time. The role of the financial sector in fostering development has also been the subject of much analysis (see, for example, Levine [1997]).

More recently, economists have attempted to uncover the "deeper" determinants of economic growth that exercise their influence over long periods of time (see Table 4.4). The following factors have been identified as possibly fundamental:

- Geography (Mellinger, Sachs, and Gallup 2000; Sachs 2001). Many of the poorest countries are located near the equator. Countries in the tropic regions generally possess less fertile soil, unstable water supplies, and a larger incidence of diseases and other adverse conditions which impede their development. In ad-

Table 4.3 Shares of World GDP (%)

	1870	1913	1950	1973	2003
Western Europe	33.1	33.0	26.2	25.6	19.2
U.S., Canada, Australia, NZ	10.0	21.3	30.6	25.3	23.7
Asia	38.3	24.9	18.6	24.2	40.5
Latin America	2.5	4.4	7.8	8.7	7.7
Eastern Europe & USSR	12.0	13.4	13.1	12.8	5.7
Africa	4.1	2.9	3.8	3.4	3.2

SOURCE: Maddison (2007).

dition, those countries that are landlocked face higher transportation costs and less access to foreign goods and ideas.

- Economic openness (Frankel and Romer 1999; Sachs and Warner 1995). Economies that are integrated with the world economy are open to technological advances, have the opportunity to specialize in the production of goods, and can take advantage of economies of scale. Many of the fastest-growing East Asian economies have used international trade to accelerate their growth.

- Institutions (Knack and Keefer 1995; North 1990). These are the rules and practices, both formal and informal, that govern behavior. The institutions that promote property rights and an effective legal system encourage innovation by their inhabitants. The quality of governance provides an assurance of stability.

Empirical researchers have sought to distinguish the relative importance of these factors in the determination and variation of income over time. This task is complicated by their interrelationships: geography, for example, can affect a country's integration with the global economy and the evolution of its institutions. There can also be feedback between economic openness and the development of institutions. In order to isolate the effect of the different proposed determinants, economists look for instrumental variables that are exogenously correlated with economic integration or institutions, but not the other possible determinants of income, to test their relationships with output.

Acemoglu, Johnson, and Robinson (2001), for example, use the mortality rates of European settlers in their colonies to explain the vari-

Table 4.4 Sources of Low Growth Rates

Source	Transmission mechanisms	Authors
Geography	Soil fertility Water availability Health	Mellinger, Sachs, and Gallup (2000) Sachs (2001)
Economic openness	Economies of scale Technological innovation	Sachs and Warner (1995) Frankel and Romer (1999)
Institutions	Property rights Quality of governance	North (1990) Knack and Keefer (1995)

ation in institutions. They reason that colonies that were located in areas with high disease rates were more likely to be "extractive states" where the colonizers sought to obtain natural resources with little development of supportive institutions. Colonies with better health conditions, however, were more likely to be settled by Europeans who sought to replicate the institutions they had left behind. These early conditions influenced the evolution of institutions after the colonies achieved independence. Using this identification strategy, Acemoglu, Johnson, and Robinson examine the determinants of per capita GDP in 1995 in 64 countries, and report that institutional development had a positive and statistically significant impact: countries with better institutions had higher income levels. Geography and health conditions, on the other hand, were not significant.

Similarly, Easterly and Levine (2003) undertake tests of the determinants of per capita GDP in 72 countries using variables such as settler mortality rates to explain institutional development. They report evidence in favor of the hypothesis that institutions play a direct causal role in the determination of real per capita output. They also find that geographical factors only influence growth indirectly through their impact on institutions. In a third paper, Rodrik, Subramanian, and Trebbi (2004) report that the quality of institutions "trumps" the other possible determinants of income, including openness and integration.

While no consensus ever remains unchallenged, these studies produce consistent results. The World Bank (2005) has summarized the findings of this body of research: "Recent econometric and case studies have shown that even when controlling for historical endogeneity, institutions remain 'deep' causal factors, while openness and geography operate at best through them" (p. 57).

INSTITUTIONAL DEVELOPMENT

The econometric evidence, therefore, indicates that differences in institutional development account for the dispersion in global income. Rodrik, Subramanian, and Trebbi (2004), however, caution that their results have limited practical guidance for those who wish to promote growth through improving the quality of institutions. They claim that "there is growing evidence that desirable institutional arrangements have a large element of context specificity, arising from differences in historical trajectories, geography, political economy, or other initial conditions" (p. 157).

In a survey of the research done on institutional development, Shirley (2005) summarizes the explanations that have been advanced for under-developed institutions, such as colonial heritages plus resources that could be exploited by colonizers who designed institutions to appropri-ate these resources; a lack of political competition, which would have placed constraints on political powers; and beliefs and norms that were not hospitable to the formation of institutions (p. 617). The proximate historical causes of institutional development, on the other hand, are greater equality combined with sufficient political competition to limit the ability of rulers to expropriate, combined with long periods of time (p. 625).

Shirley (2005) also supports Rodrik, Subramanian, and Trebbi's (2004) point that the development of institutions depends on domestic conditions. She cites several examples where the transfer of existing institutions from one country to another failed to take root, including the experience of Latin American countries with the U.S. constitution and the record of the transition economies with U.S. and European bankruptcy laws and commercial codes. She cites the need for what Levy and Spiller (1994) call a "goodness of fit" between specific insti-tutional changes and a country's overall environment.

Outside agents, such as the intergovernmental organizations, have become aware of the need for good institutions for progress to be made in fostering growth and alleviating poverty. The World Bank undertakes extensive research on this topic and maintains databases on the qual-ity of governance and institutions. The World Bank's *World Develop-ment Report 2002*, for example, was subtitled *Building Institutions for Markets*. But Shirley (2005) is pessimistic about the ability of foreign organizations to induce institutional improvement, since most insti-tutional changes take place over longer time frames than the horizon of aid projects. Honda (2008) studies the impact of IMF programs on economic governance and finds no evidence of a significant impact for nonconcessional lending. Only the IMF's concessional lending to the poorest countries had a significant impact on improving the rule of law and the control of corruption.

Another cautionary note comes from the literature on the impact of foreign aid on governance and development. Knack (2001) reports that higher aid levels had a negative impact on the quality of governance. Easterly (2006) has written extensively about the failures of foreign-financed development projects to improve economic performance in the countries where they have taken place. Burnside and Dollar (2000) seem to have found a solution when they report evidence that aid was effective if the recipient countries had implemented good macroeconomic and trade policies. But Easterly, Levine, and Roodman (2004) find that those results were not robust to the addition of new countries and observations to the original data set.

However, there may be long-term links between globalization and governance over time. Wei (2000), for example, looks at the impact of what he terms "natural openness," that is, the level of trade openness that a country should have based on its size, geographic location, and linguistic characteristics. He finds a negative and significant linkage between natural openness and the prevalence of corruption, as measured by Business International and Transparency International corruption indexes. Wei attributes this linkage to decisions by more open economies to promote good governance and minimize corruption in order to advance their trade with other countries. He suggests that the process of globalization would provide similar incentives to other economies.

Bonaglia, de Macedo, and Bussolo (2001) also examine the impact of openness (imports/GDP) on corruption, as measured by the Transparency International and the International Country Risk Guide, and find that countries with a higher degree of openness record lower levels of corruption. They caution, however, that reducing trade barriers may not bring an immediate reduction in corruption, and that domestic policies may be more important in the short run. Similarly, Al-Marhubi (2004) finds that countries that are more open have better governance.

The IMF (2005), in an analysis of the determinants of institutional transitions, finds that trade openness is associated with a greater likelihood of improved institutions. The authors attribute this to less corruption in the export sector and the reduction of the ability of domestic producers to sustain monopolistic rents, which could be used to influence governments. They also find that transitions are more likely to occur when they also take place in neighboring countries.

But international trade can also have negative effects on the development of good institutions. Pogge (2002, 2005) points out that the sale of natural resources can support dictatorial regimes. First, the existence of such resources is an incentive for civil strife, as the winner can take control of state-owned properties, including publicly owned resources. Second, the revenues received by an unrepresentative government allow it to remain in power, even in the face of dissent.

Saudi Arabia, for example, received scores of 7 and 6 on the Freedom House 2007 ratings for political rights and civil liberties, where the ratings range from 1 (highest degree of freedom) to 7 (lowest).[4] The government's ability to remain in power rests in part on its oil revenues, which it uses to distribute services to the population. The dependence of energy consumers in the upper-income countries on foreign oil contributes to the Saudi government's survival.

Globalization in earlier eras may have played a role in how institutions evolved in those countries that were colonies. The maps of modern Africa and other areas were drawn by their former colonial powers when they existed. These national lines often ignored domestic ethnic divisions and other historical factors. The resulting geographic divisions were not consistent with past governing structures, and as a result domestic governments did not have a unified basis of support within their populations. An even more invidious cause of underdevelopment has been suggested by Nunn (2008), who finds evidence of a link between African poverty and slavery. He finds that those countries that were the major sources of slaves now are among the poorest, and suggests that the underdevelopment of political structures in the major slave-exporters may be a reason for this linkage.

GLOBALIZATION AND THE POOR

Even if institutions determine the level of economic activity in the long run, globalization can still have an impact on the poorer nations. The primary channel of transmission is the impact of globalization upon growth, and the evidence generally confirms that open economies grow faster and see a decline in the incidence of poverty (see Dollar and Kraay 2004). The World Bank (2005) finds that growth was responsible for almost all the significant reductions in poverty in the 1990s, including those that occurred in China and India.

However, the implications of this finding are the subject of much debate and controversy. In the 1980s, many policymakers and analysts believed that removing barriers to international trade and capital flows, as well as lifting regulations on interest rates and other market-oriented measures, would lead to faster growth. Many of these recommended policy measures were summarized by Williamson (1990) as the "Washington Consensus."[5] The experience of the East Asian economies that had grown so rapidly was cited as proof that integration with the global economy would raise growth in developing countries.

But the record of the 1990s raised questions about the results of removing financial barriers. The financial crises that occurred, for example, in Mexico in 1994–1995, East Asia in 1997–1998, and Argentina in 2001 severely depressed the standard of living in those countries. Baldacci, de Mello, and Inchauste (2002) have reported that such financial crises are linked to an increase in poverty and income inequality.

These crises showed that short-term capital outflows could seriously disrupt the economies of countries such as Thailand and Indonesia, which had removed controls on capital flows. On the other hand, China and India, both of which maintained capital controls, were relatively unscathed by the crisis. Malaysia imposed capital controls during the crisis in 1998 to slow the flight of capital. While there were concerns at the time that the country had cut itself off from future international investments, its economy revived and international capital flows resumed.

Subsequently, there was a reaction to what was called the "market fundamentalism" of the earlier period, particularly with respect to capital flows. The recent U.S. subprime mortgage crisis shows that even financial institutions in developed countries engage in risky transactions that can become full-blown crises. The IMF, which had previously encouraged its members to dismantle capital controls, revised its approach (see Joyce and Noy [2008]). The Fund now emphasizes the sequencing of reforms before financial globalization in order to minimize financial sector instability. The reform measures include " . . . the development of financial markets and institutions; prudential regulation and supervision; risk management and good practices in accounting, auditing, and disclosure; and financial safety nets" (IMF 2002, p. 3).

The impact of trade liberalization on the poorest nations is usually seen as more favorable, particularly for those that export agricultural goods. However, deregulation can affect some groups within a country, such as those who might pay higher food prices. Winters, McCulloch, and McKay (2004) review the evidence for all the linkages between trade liberalization and poverty, and present a carefully worded appraisal: "Theory provides a strong presumption that trade liberalization will be poverty-alleviating in the long-run and on average. The empirical evidence broadly supports this view, and, in particular, lends no support to the position that trade liberalization generally has an adverse impact. Equally, however, it does not assert that trade policy is always among the most important determinants of poverty reduction or that the static and micro-economic effects of liberalization will always be beneficial for the poor" (p. 107).

The impact of globalization on poverty and inequality, therefore, is far from settled, either among economists or the wider public. Aisbett (2007), who studies criticisms made of globalization, points out that " . . . much work remains to show which policies can reduce the adjustment costs borne by the poor and maximize the share of the benefits they obtain from globalization" (p. 67). Bardhan (2006), who examines the linkages between poverty and globalization, concludes, " . . . globalization is not the main cause of developing countries' problems, contrary to the claim of critics of globalization—just as globalization is often not the main solution to these problems, contrary to the claim of overenthusiastic free traders" (p. 90).

MANAGING GLOBALIZATION

Can globalization be managed to play a positive role in ending poverty? Rodrik (2007) agrees with those who believe that growth is the most powerful mechanism to reduce poverty and that globalization provides opportunities for increasing growth rates. However, he also has pointed out that there are many different ways to achieve growth, and governments need to choose the policies and institutions appropriate for their nations to take advantage of the opportunities of globalization. His calls for pragmatism and experimentation are similar to the views of Easterly (2006), who criticizes outside attempts to impose solutions on countries.

Are there steps the upper-income countries could take that would help the poor countries? Birdsall, Rodrik, and Subramanian (2005) warn that some of the proposed measures, such as liberalizing trade, may not have the impact that their advocates envision. Many of the poorest countries, for example, are importers of agricultural products, and removing the subsidies paid to the agricultural sector within the United States and the European Union would only raise prices on those products at a time when world food prices are already rapidly rising (Economist 2008).

On the other hand, Birdsall, Rodrik, and Subramanian (2005) also point to concrete steps that would make the international economy more rewarding for poor countries. First, they claim that the upper-income nations can promote good institutions by monitoring and restricting the payments of bribes to officials in developing nations. Second, they propose that the governments of the wealthy countries promote research on issues and problems most relevant to the global poor but which their own governments cannot afford. One way to accomplish this would be to guarantee the purchase from private companies of technological innovations that benefit the poor. Finally, the current regulations that govern international migration should be overhauled. The governments of countries that attract migrants can collaborate with the governments of their home countries to devise contract labor schemes that allow workers to enter the host country for some period of time, benefitting both countries.

Globalization will continue, with benefits for countries that may not have participated in the global economy to date. The World Bank (2007) estimates that the share of developing countries in global output will increase from about one-fifth to one-third by 2030. Similarly, it forecasts that the global trade of goods and services will rise by three times to approximately $27 trillion in 2030, and half of that increase will come from developing nations.

However, the World Bank (2007) warns that the benefits of increased economic integration are likely to be uneven across different areas. In addition, the prevalence of inequality within nations may rise. "[S]trong forces in the global economy may tend to increase inequality in many national economies. Even though a large segment of the developing world is likely to enter what can be called the 'global middle class,' some social groups may be left behind or even marginalized in the growth process" (p. xvi).

Managing the process of globalization to benefit the maximum number of people and diminish the gap in incomes across nations, therefore, is a challenge for all nations. This challenge has been exacerbated by the downturn in world trade and capital flows during the global financial crisis. How governments and intergovernmental organizations respond will determine whether that gap diminishes or grows larger over time.

Notes

1. These figures are taken from Maddison (2007) and are calculated in 1990 international dollars.
2. These data are obtained from the *World Development Indicators* and are calculated in constant 2000 dollars.
3. Weil (2008) provides a comprehensive review of this subject.
4. See http://www.freedomhouse.org.
5. However, Williamson (1990) does not include the removal of controls on all capital inflows.

References

Acemoglu, Daron, Simon Johnson, and James A. Robinson. 2001. "The Colonial Origins of Comparative Development: An Empirical Investigation." *American Economic Review* 91(5): 1369–1401.

Aisbett, Emma. 2007. "Why Are the Critics So Convinced that Globalization Is Bad for the Poor?" In *Globalization and Poverty*, Ann Harrison, ed. Chicago: University of Chicago Press, pp. 33–75.

Al-Marhubi, Fahim. 2004. "The Determinants of Governance: A Cross-Country Analysis." *Contemporary Economic Policy* 2(3): 394–406.

Baldacci, Emanuele, Luiz de Mello, and Gabriela Inchauste. 2002. "Financial Crises, Poverty, and Income Distribution." IMF Working Paper No. 02/4. Washington, DC: International Monetary Fund.

Bardhan, Pranab. 2006. "Does Globalization Help or Hurt the World's Poor?" *Scientific American* 294(4): 84–91.

Barro, Robert. 1997. *Determinants of Economic Growth*. Cambridge, MA, and London: MIT Press.

Birdsall, Nancy, Dani Rodrik, and Arvind Subramanian. 2005. "How to Help Poor Countries." *Foreign Affairs* 84(4): 136–152.

Bonaglia, Federico, Jorge Braga de Macedo, and Maurizio Bussolo. 2001. "How Globalization Improves Governance." CEPR Discussion Paper No. 2992. London: Centre for Economic Policy Research.

Burnside, Craig, and David Dollar. 2000. "Aid, Policies, and Growth." *American Economic Review* 40(2): 847–868.

Dollar, David, and Aart Kraay. 2004. "Trade, Growth, and Poverty." *Economic Journal* 114(493): F22–F49.

Easterly, William. 2006. *The White Man's Burden: Why the West's Efforts to Aid the Rest Have Done So Much Ill and So Little Good.* New York: Penguin Press.

Easterly, William, and Ross Levine. 2003. "Tropics, Germs, and Crops: How Endowments Influence Economic Development." *Journal of Monetary Economics* 50(1): 3–39.

Easterly, William, Ross Levine, and David Roodman. 2004. "Aid, Policies, and Growth: Comment." *American Economic Review* 94(3): 774–780.

Economist. 2008. "Briefing: Food and the Poor: The New Face of Hunger." 387(8576): 30.

Frankel, Jeffrey A., and David Romer. 1999. "Does Trade Cause Growth?" *American Economic Review* 89(3): 379–399.

Honda, Jiro. 2008. "Do IMF Programs Improve Economic Governance?" IMF Working Paper No. 08/114. Washington, DC: International Monetary Fund.

International Monetary Fund. 2002. *Capital Account Liberalization and Financial Sector Stability.* Occasional Paper No. 211. Washington, DC: IMF.

———. 2005. *World Economic Outlook.* Washington, DC: IMF.

Joyce, Joseph P., and Ilan Noy. 2008. "The IMF and the Liberalization of Capital Controls." *Review of International Economics* 16(3): 413–430.

Knack, Stephen. 2001. "Aid Dependence and the Quality of Governance: Cross-Country Empirical Tests." *Southern Economic Journal* 68(2): 310–329.

Knack, Stephen, and Philip Keefer. 1995. "Institutions and Economic Performance: Cross-Country Tests Using Alternative Institutional Measures." *Economics & Politics* 7(3): 207–227.

Levine, Ross. 1997. "Financial Development and Economic Growth: Views and Agenda." *Journal of Economic Literature* 35(2): 688–726.

Levy, Brian, and Pablo T. Spiller. 1994. *Regulations, Institutions, and Commitment: Comparative Studies of Telecommunications.* Cambridge, MA, and New York: Cambridge University Press.

Maddison, Angus. 2007. *Contours of the World Economy, 1–2030 AD: Essays in Macro-Economic History.* Oxford and New York: Oxford University Press.

Mellinger, Andrew D., Jeffrey D. Sachs, and John L. Gallup. 2000. "Climate,

Coastal Proximity and Development." In *Oxford Handbook of Economic Geography*, Gordon L. Clark, Maryann P. Feldman, and Meric S. Gertler, eds. Oxford and New York: Oxford University Press, pp. 169–194.

North, Douglas C. 1990. *Institutions, Institutional Change and Economic Performance.* Cambridge, UK, and New York: Cambridge University Press.

Nunn, Nathan. 2008. "The Long-Term Effects of Africa's Slave Trades." *Quarterly Journal of Economics* 123(1): 139–176.

Nussbaum, Martha. 2006. *Frontiers of Justice: Disability, Nationality, Species Membership.* Cambridge, MA, and London: Belknap Press.

Pogge, Thomas. 2002. *World Poverty and Human Rights.* Cambridge, UK, and Malden, MA: Polity.

———. 2005. "World Poverty and Human Rights." *Ethics & International Affairs.* 19(1): 1–7.

Rawls, John. 1999. *The Law of Peoples.* Cambridge, MA: Harvard University Press.

Risse, Mathias. 2005a. "Do We Owe the Global Poor Assistance or Rectification?" *Ethics & International Affairs* 19(1): 9–54.

———. 2005b. "How Does the Global Order Harm the Poor?" *Philosophy and Public Affairs* 33(4): 349–376.

———. 2005c. "What We Owe to the Global Poor." *Journal of Ethics* 9(1–2): 81–117.

Rodrik, Dani. 2007. *One Economics, Many Recipes: Globalization, Institutions, and Economic Growth.* Princeton, NJ: Princeton University Press.

Rodrik, Dani, Arvind Subramanian, and Francesco Trebbi. 2004. "Institutions Rule: The Primacy of Institutions over Geography and Integration in Economic Development." *Journal of Economic Growth* 9(2): 131–165.

Sachs, Jeffrey. 2001. "Tropical Underdevelopment." NBER Working Paper No. 8119. Cambridge, MA: National Bureau of Economic Research.

Sachs, Jeffrey, and Andrew Warner. 1995. "Economic Reform and the Process of Global Integration." *Brookings Papers on Economic Activity* 195(1): 827–838.

Shirley, Mary M. 2005. "Institutions and Development." In *Handbook of New Institutional Economics*, Claude Menard and Mary M. Shirley, eds. Dordrecht and New York: Springer, pp. 611–638.

Wei, Shang-Jin. 2000. "Natural Openness and Good Governance." NBER Working Paper No. 7765. Cambridge, MA: National Bureau of Economic Research.

Weil, David. 2008. *Economic Growth.* 2nd ed. Boston: Addison Wesley.

Williamson, John. 1990. "What Washington Means by Policy Reform." In *Latin American Readjustment: How Much Has Happened*, John Williamson, ed. Washington, DC: Institute for International Economics, pp. 5–20.

Winters, L. Alan, Neil McCulloch, and Andrew McKay. 2004. "Trade Liberalization and Poverty: The Evidence So Far." *Journal of Economic Literature* 42(1): 72–115.

World Bank. 2005. *Economic Growth in the 1990s: Learning from a Decade of Reform.* Washington, DC: World Bank.

———. 2007. *Global Economic Prospects: Managing the Next Wave of Globalization.* Washington, DC: World Bank.

5

The Composition and Allocation of Global Financial Flows

What Are Markets Doing?

Linda Tesar
University of Michigan

This chapter focuses on global financial flows and how they have changed in response to the series of financial crises that swept through emerging markets in the mid- to late 1990s. There have been some significant changes in the direction and the composition of capital flow, and this chapter argues that some of those changes can be understood as the response of markets to fundamental weaknesses in the global financial system—weaknesses that have not been adequately addressed by multilateral institutions or by individual governments.

Development is fundamentally about moving resources to the places where they are needed most. Somehow the movement of those resources needs to be financed, whether as outright transfers, through loans, through direct investment in foreign corporations, or through securities markets. The nature of development finance has changed dramatically over time, and we have learned, sometimes through painful experience, about how the composition of capital flow from rich to poor countries matters. While the composition of capital flow is by definition a "macro" phenomenon, I suggest that micro evidence on the way firms structure their lending to emerging markets contains important clues about the vulnerabilities of the global financial environment, and how firms have responded to those weaknesses.

The financial crises that swept through East Asia and Latin America in the mid- to late 1990s interrupted global flows, but one feature that stands out is the resilience of, and even the expansion of, foreign direct investment (FDI) flows. One can think of the policy reforms applied to emerging markets in two phases: first as the "Washington Consensus

I," which emphasized getting prices right (the Washington Consensus is explained further in the following section). We learned from financial crises that getting prices right is not enough, and there is a new perspective that I have labeled "Washington Consensus II," which is about getting institutions right. The world made progress with phase I, the opening of markets, but has been less successful with phase II. Failure to adequately address institutions has not stopped capital flow, but it has changed the nature of that flow.

GLOBAL FINANCIAL FLOWS AND THE WASHINGTON CONSENSUS

Historically, flows to developing countries moved through official channels—from multilateral agencies or governments to recipient governments. Bank lending and FDI played a role, but official flows accounted for the majority of capital flow to developing countries. In the 1990s, the composition of capital flow began to shift away from official assistance toward private capital flow. Much of this shift was due to the dramatic changes in policy that occurred under the "Washington Consensus," a term coined by John Williamson (2002) at the Institute for International Economics. It was a convenient label for the broad set of policies supported by the U.S. Treasury and the IMF for reforming economies in emerging markets.

The Washington Consensus covered three broad areas, the first of which was that developing countries should have greater macroeconomic discipline, including a reduction in fiscal deficits, reprioritization of expenditures, and tax reform. The second major component was to encourage policies that foster the market economy to liberalize interest rates, liberalize the banking system, deregulate financial institutions, privatize government-run enterprises, and encourage greater securitization. In other words, the reforms were intended to create a greater role for market-determined prices to affect allocations. One of the key prices in small open economies is the exchange rate, although the debate still ensues today about the best way to manage exchange rates.

Finally, the consensus supported opening the economy to the global marketplace through trade liberalization and, to some extent, capital account liberalization. *Ex post*, there is now a heated debate about whether capital account liberalization is a good idea and if so, how it should best be accomplished, but *ex ante*, many economists believed that emerging market economies would benefit from lifting restrictions on the extent of foreign control, allowing foreigners to become shareholders in local firms and encouraging the entry of foreign banks. In response to pressure from the IMF and other institutions, many countries undertook massive privatization programs and liberalized their capital markets. These privatization programs took place in conjunction with the removal of capital account restrictions that permitted increased market access to foreign investors.

Economists predicted that such reforms would generate a number of benefits for emerging markets. Economic theory suggests that opening to global financial markets should stimulate the flow of capital from capital-rich to capital-poor countries and reduce the cost of capital in markets where it is scarce. The reforms should increase the efficiency of the financial sector and facilitate the transfer of technology. A second-order effect is to help diversify risk by reducing local investors' exposure to country-specific risk. At a minimum, these reforms, even if they do not change the long-run growth rate, would speed the transition to the country's long-run steady state by an inflow of foreign capital. The more optimistic view is that financial liberalization and openness could potentially increase economic growth rates.

Many countries took this policy advice and opened their markets. The number of countries with stock markets open to foreign investors increased from 14 in 1980 (essentially the largest OECD countries) to 35 in 1992, leveling off to 41 in the late 1990s (Bekaert, Harvey, and Lundblad 2005). Chinn and Ito (2006) develop an alternative measure of openness, taking into account policy differences across countries in the various components of the capital account (see Figure 5.1). Their measure captures the opening of the capital accounts, particularly in Latin America and East Europe.[1]

Net resource flows to developing countries, and most notably flows to emerging markets, increased dramatically from the early 1980s to the mid-1990s (see Figure 5.2). If we strategically stop time in 1997, it appears that capital flow responded as economists predicted it would: with a quadrupling of total flow from $75 billion in 1990 to over $300 billion in 1997. Looking at flows by type, FDI followed a similar path,

Figure 5.1 Chinn-Ito Financial Openness Index

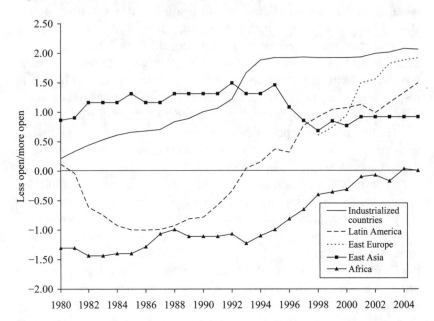

SOURCE: Chinn and Ito (2006).

increasing from less than $50 billion to more than $150 billion over the same period. International investment in portfolio equity, which was virtually nonexistent in the 1980s, accounted for an increasing share of capital flow in the early 1990s. At its peak in 1993, equity flows accounted for 20 percent of total capital inflow in developing countries.

Privatization and increased foreign investment led to a boom in emerging stock markets. The growth in stock market capitalization of emerging markets, which reflects the increase in the number of firms listed on the market as well as the change in stock prices, was a staggering 250 percent over the 1990–1996 period. The U.S. equity market, enjoying its own stock market boom over this period, grew about 170 percent, with slower rates of growth in the United Kingdom and Japan. Foreign markets, particularly emerging markets, looked like a good investment, and U.S. investors responded. Home bias, measured as the

Figure 5.2 Net Resource Flows to Developing Countries, 1980–2005

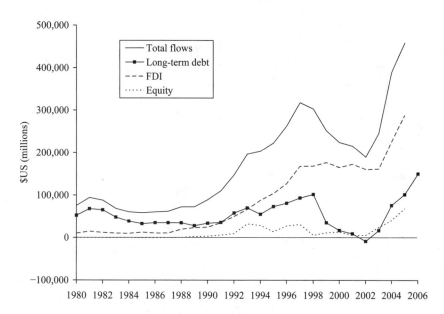

SOURCE: *Global Development Finance*, World Bank.

fraction of U.S. equities in the U.S. portfolio, declined from 97 percent in the 1980s to about 88 percent in 1995.

Despite the increased flows to developing markets, international capital markets were still dominated by flows between industrialized countries. Of the total global outflow of FDI of $322 billion in 1995, 94 percent, or $302 billion, was invested in industrialized countries. Similarly, 96 percent of outward investment in portfolio equity was invested in industrialized countries. So, while there was some seepage of global flows into developing countries, the volume of that flow remained relatively small.

Capital markets also did not deliver on the promise of redistributing wealth from the rich to the poor. A Lorenz curve of the distribution of wealth for 59 countries, which shows the fraction of global wealth accounted for by each decile of countries ranked by wealth, shows very little change between 1970 and 1995 (Figure 5.3). Wealth here includes

Figure 5.3　Lorenz Curve for Global Wealth, 1970 and 1995

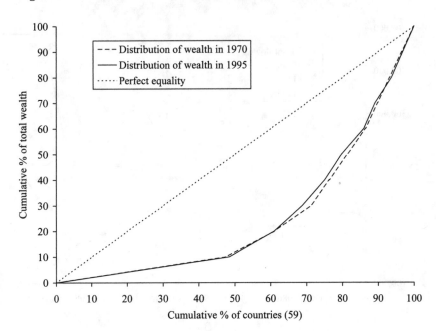

SOURCE: Author's calculations based on net foreign asset and liability data reported by Lane and Milesi-Ferretti (2001).

the capitalized value of a country's capital stock as well as its stock of foreign assets. If wealth were distributed approximately evenly, the poorest 10 percent of countries would have 10 percent of global wealth. (If the distribution were exactly equal, the Lorenz curve would lie along the 45 degree line and there would be no distinction between the rich and the poor.) The data suggest that 10 percent of global wealth is shared by the bottom 50 percent of countries. These figures are an underestimate of the uneven distribution of wealth, because the sample excludes most of sub-Saharan Africa, the poorest countries in Asia, and Eastern Europe because of the lack of information on capital stocks and net foreign assets in those regions.

Even if one thought that wealth might not be affected by the opening of capital markets, one would hope that the allocation of capital would be affected. That is, open capital markets would encourage investment in capital-scarce countries even if ownership of that capital, and therefore wealth, remained in the hands of investors in industrialized countries. Unfortunately, the data suggest that there was also very little change in the distribution of capital across countries between 1970 and 1995. In 1995, the richest 50 percent of countries accounted for 85 percent of the global capital stock.

Of course, the clock did not stop in the mid-1990s, and beginning with the Mexican crisis in December 1994, global markets were buffeted with a series of financial shocks that seemed to spread from one market to the next. These crises resulted in (or some would say were caused by) a sudden reversal of capital flow from emerging markets, speculative attacks on fixed exchange rates and the central banks that supported them, collapses in the financial sectors of many Latin American and Southeast Asian countries, liquidity crises, and ultimately widespread defaults. The cause of these crises remains a topic of heated discussion and is beyond the scope of this chapter.

The "sudden stop" in capital flow to emerging markets resulted in a dramatic reduction in total flows to developing countries, from a peak of $310 billion in 1997 to less than $200 billion in 2001. Flows of long-term debt fell in 1999 and became negative in 2001. Portfolio equity flows were reduced to a trickle. Interestingly, while the other types of flow declined, FDI remained steady from 1997 on and took a sharp turn upward in 2003. This is seen even more clearly when one looks at the decomposition of flows by type (i.e., as a percentage of total flow). Throughout the entire 1980–2001 period, FDI as a fraction of total inflow steadily increased, and by 2001 it accounted for 80 percent of the total volume of flow to developing countries. The remainder of the chapter examines why, and how one should think about FDI flows in this environment.

To understand FDI flows, it helps to make the distinction between greenfield investments, the inflow of new investments, and "brownfield" investments, mergers and acquisitions (M&As) that reflect the purchase of existing plants and equipment. Throughout the late 1990s the fraction of FDI that is accounted for by the acquisition of firms in emerging markets by firms in industrialized countries increased. In 1999, over 90 percent of FDI in Asia was due to cross-border M&As.

The rise in cross-border M&As as a form of external finance was in part due to changes in the regulations affecting foreign ownership.

In many countries in East Asia, foreign investors were explicitly pro-hibited from gaining a controlling share in local firms. For example, in 1996 the ceiling on the amount of stock foreigners could acquire in all Korean companies without the approval of the board of directors was only 18 percent. Another feature of the market for corporate control in Korea was that cross-holdings across business groups (Chaebols) were substantial. This situation changed dramatically as a consequence of the financial crises that swept the region during 1997. The IMF bailout packages to Thailand, Korea, and Indonesia included explicit provi-sions for restructuring domestic capital markets and to allow foreign competition in the market for corporate control.

Another feature of FDI inflows is that they are lumpy; that is, a single transaction in a small market can have a huge impact on aggre-gate flow. Argentina is an interesting example. In 1999, forecasts about Argentina's near economic future and the viability of its currency board were grim. Debt flows steeply declined and portfolio inflows turned negative. Foreign direct investment, however, surged upward to unprec-edented levels. A careful look at the data reveals that the sale of YPF, an oil and gas company, to Repsol, a Spanish enterprise, accounted for 63 percent of total FDI inflow in that year. Had Repsol not made the purchase, net flows to Argentina would have been close to zero.

The next question is how to interpret the boom in foreign acquisi-tions in emerging markets. Many views in the press range from firms now having access to the "exciting opportunities" in emerging markets, to a fire sale of assets resulting from the liquidity crises, to the fear of "recolonization" by foreign entities (the latter is attributed to Malaysia's Prime Minister Mahathir). Economists also express a range of opinions, from FDI as the "good cholesterol" (borrowing may not be good for you, but if you have to do it FDI is the least dangerous form) to a more neutral perspective (FDI is simply the transfer of assets from domestic to foreign hands and therefore may have little real economic impact) to a more positive view that FDI enables the transfer of technology and creates synergies between parents and their affiliates.

To try to shed light on the factors that drive cross-border M&As, I explore three questions. First, is there value creation from the transfer of assets from domestic to foreign hands? Second, if there is value cre-ation, who captures the gains—targets in emerging markets or acquir-ers from industrialized countries? And finally, are there special circumstances under which gains exist, and why? To get at these questions, I will use the stock price reaction of acquirer and target firms to the announcement of an M&A transaction as a summary statistic for the value created through cross-border M&A activity.

The results in this chapter are drawn from Chari, Ouimet, and Tesar (2009). The returns are cumulated average abnormal returns over a three-day event window around the announcement date.[2] Our data set includes all acquisitions of firms in 42 emerging markets in Africa, Asia, and Latin America by firms from nine industrialized countries. The sample period covers 1986–2006, making it possible to test for the effects of financial crisis on the gains from an acquisition. The data set includes various firm, industry, and transactions characteristics. We also have data for a control group that includes domestic and other industrialized-country acquisitions by U.S. and European firms. This allows us to compare the gains from acquiring a target in an emerging market relative to the gains from acquiring a target in another industrialized country.

Our analysis yields three main findings. First, there is value creation from cross-border M&As in emerging markets. Between 1986 and 2006, developed market acquirers experienced positive and significant abnormal returns of 1.16 percent, on average, over a three-day event window.

Our second finding is that shareholders of acquiring firms reap the lion's share of the gains, and this gain is associated with acquiring control. The median acquirer records cumulative abnormal returns of 0.72 percent in transactions where control is acquired, while the median cumulative abnormal return for acquirers in transactions where control is not acquired is 0.02 percent. Over the period we study, the cumulated dollar value gain from cross-border acquisitions in emerging markets where control was acquired was $10.5 billion for developed market shareholders. Note that this is in stark contrast to the results from the domestic M&A literature where studies find that M&As are value destroying and that the gains, if any, accrue to the target's shareholders (Moeller, Schlingemann, and Stulz 2005). This suggests that something very different is going on in the emerging market context. The effect appears to be closely related to corporate control.

Finally, we find that the gains for acquirers are largest in R&D intensive sectors, conditional on gaining control. To obtain this result, we first estimate R&D intensity at the industry level based on a cross-section of U.S. industries. We then use those estimates as a measure of R&D intensity of targets (by industry). When we include this measure of R&D intensity as a control variable in the regression, we find that corporate control, crossed with R&D intensity, is a significant explanator of acquirer gains. One interpretation of this finding is that there are productive synergies from M&As that involve the transfer of technology, but these synergies are only realized (and the technology is transferred) when the acquirer obtains control.

How can we interpret these findings? In *Financial Crisis, Liquidity and the International Monetary Problem*, Jean Tirole (2001) offers insight into the potential causes of market failure in emerging markets that has direct bearing on the decision to acquire a foreign firm. First, he assumes that there are many lenders, and that lenders do not coordinate their actions. On the borrowing side, he assumes that the local government can take actions that affect the payoffs of the firm, and that the incentives of the government are not fully aligned with those of the firm. Two problems then arise. First, the lack of coordination among lenders means that each lender is uncertain about the borrowing country's overall level of indebtedness, and each lender is uncertain about the relative seniority of his or her own claim. This situation can lead to sunspot equilibria, speculative attacks, and contagion as each investor tries to infer from inexact signals whether or not his or her claim will be honored. The second problem is that lenders would like to contract with the firm, but the government is an implicit partner in the arrangement. Thus, the lender is exposed to expropriation risk; that is, actions that are not in the best interest of the firm.

Foreign direct investment, in the form of acquiring control of the emerging market firm, offers a way out of these two problems. By contracting explicitly with the shareholders of the target firm, FDI essentially cuts out other lenders (minimizing the multiple lender problem). In gaining majority ownership of the firm, shareholders of the acquiring firm are able to extend the boundary of the firm into the emerging market, effectively replacing the government of the target-firm nation with that of the acquirer. This is not to say that all expropriation risk is eliminated—the target's government could still violate international law, for example, and nationalize the target. But by consolidating the balance sheets of the target and the acquirer, the acquisition effectively extends the reach of the acquirer's home institutions into the borrower's market. In a sense, the target imports the corporate and legal institutions from the acquirer.

Foreign direct investment is not, however, a panacea for the weak institutions problem plaguing emerging markets. It is relatively immobile, may be inflexible, and may not help a country diversify its risk. It also comes at a price. In order to attract FDI and to compensate for the weak institutions problem, target shareholders in emerging markets give up both control and, relative to target shareholders in industrial countries, returns. The only complete solution is for governments in emerging markets to address the weaknesses in their contracting environment, to offer greater property rights protection, and to make firms less vulnerable to capricious changes in government policy.

Another recent phenomenon, which I believe is also a symptom of the weak institutions problem, is the dramatic rise in foreign reserve accumulation in developing countries. According to neoclassical theory, capital-scarce countries should be net borrowers, not net lenders. Yet what we see is the accumulation of large holdings of dollar reserves by foreign governments, particularly in developing countries. Economists continue to debate about the explanation of these reserve holdings, but one plausible explanation is that in a world where financial meltdowns are a possibility, foreign reserves serve as collateral and provide a signal to foreign investors that the countries' balance sheets are sound.

SUMMARY

The composition of global financial flows to emerging markets changed dramatically in the postfinancial crisis period. External finance is now much more likely to take the form of the sale of domestic assets, with control rights shifting to the acquiring firm. In my view, this change in the composition of flows is a natural response to institutional weaknesses in emerging markets. Control of foreign subsidiaries allows for both capital flow and for the protection of property rights of the acquiring firm, but it is not a perfect substitute for strong institutions that would extend to all firms in emerging markets.

Notes

1. For more details on their index, see Chinn and Ito (2006).
2. Our working paper includes robustness checks for different windows around the announcement date.

References

Bekaert, G., C. Harvey, and C. Lundblad. 2005. "Does Financial Liberalization Spur Growth?" *Journal of Financial Economics* 77(1): 3–55.

Chari, A., P. Ouimet, and L. Tesar. 2009. "The Value of Control in Emerging Markets." *Review of Financial Studies* 21(2): 605–648.

Chinn, M., and H. Ito. 2006. "What Matters for Financial Development? Capital Controls, Institutions, and Interactions." *Journal of Development Economics* 81(1): 163–192.

Global Development Finance. Various issues. Washington, DC: The World Bank.

Lane, P., and G.M. Milesi-Ferretti. 2001. "The External Wealth of Nations: Measures of Foreign Assets and Liabilities for Industrial and Developing Nations." *Journal of International Economics* 55(2): 263–294.

Moeller, S., F. Schlingemann, and R. Stulz. 2005. "Wealth Destruction on a Massive Scale? A Study of Acquiring-Firm Returns in the Recent Merger Wave." *Journal of Finance* 60(2): 757–782.

Tirole, J. 2001. *Financial Crisis, Liquidity and the International Monetary Problem*. Princeton, NJ: Princeton University Press.

Williamson, J. 2002. "Did the Washington Consensus Fail?" Speech given at the Center for Strategic and International Studies, Washington, DC, November 6.

6

Are Developing Countries Converging on Intellectual Property Rights?

Evidence from Plant Patents, 1977–2007

Lisa D. Cook
Michigan State University

For decades, researchers have attempted to develop better, more efficient sources of biofuels. On one hand, this development could represent a significant boon for developing countries. For example, sorghum in the Philippines has been found to have higher sugar content in its root than sugar cane, which is one of the best sources for efficient production of cellulosic biofuels. Economists have long advised developing countries, among others, to become less dependent on fossil fuels, whether in consumption or production. In addition, some types of biofuels may increase opportunities in production, employment, and research in the home country.

On the other hand, this could be problematic for developing countries. Provisions of the agreement on Trade-Related Aspects of Intellectual Property Rights (TRIPS) to increase protection of intellectual property rights in developing countries and emerging markets have been expensive to implement. Finger (2004) estimates that the annual cost to the least developed countries would be $60 billion. Nogués (1993) finds that Argentine pharmaceutical consumers transfer $425 million yearly to foreign patent holders. With little home-country capacity or legal framework to issue patents and protect ideas, foreign (and domestic) residents may seek greater protection abroad. Such a move could increase the price of both R&D and the use of plant varieties, reducing gains to output, employment, and R&D. Despite widespread ratification of the U.N. Convention on Biological Diversity (CBD), some developing countries argue that royalties are still underpaid due to biopiracy and bioprospecting.

How have developing countries responded to the opportunity and challenge of greater intellectual property protection? Have foreign patent offices become complements or substitutes for domestic patent offices? This chapter examines the empirical record of this response.

Using data on intellectual property related to plants, I find that there is increased activity in protecting intellectual property in and by developing countries after laws related to intellectual property are introduced. In Brazil, India, and Mexico, there is a noticeable TRIPS effect. Protected inventions increased at home and abroad after TRIPS passage in 1997. This finding implies that foreign patent offices are complements in most countries.

The chapter proceeds in four sections. The first section briefly describes the methods available to protect ideas related to plants, and the second section describes the data on intellectual property. The third section presents the evidence, and the last section describes opportunities for future research.

PROTECTION OF PLANTS

The TRIPS agreement states that "Members shall provide for the protection of plant varieties either by patents or by an effective *sui generis* system or by any combination thereof." There are four main means by which plant-related innovations may be protected: 1) patents, 2) plant breeders' rights (PBR), 3) trade secrets, and 4) trademarks.

Among patents, there are two types that are relevant for plants: utility and plant. Utility patents are granted to plant-related inventions that meet the standards of novelty, usefulness, and nonobviousness. These can either be process, such as a method of using a plant or plant part in a breeding process that includes a step of sexual hybridization, or product, such as plant, seedling, plant seed, or plant part, per se, patents.[1] According to the U.S. Patent and Trademark Office, plant patents are for products only and are granted to inventors who have "invented or discovered and asexually reproduced a distinct and new variety of plant."[2] An additional requirement is that the plant must be stable.

Among developed countries, only the United States, Japan, and Australia recognize plant patents, and no developing country recognizes them (World Bank 2006, p. 25).

The criteria for plant variety protection (PVP) are uniformity, stability, and distinctness. TRIPs compliance requires that countries offer some form of protection to breeders, and many countries selected this option. Plant variety protection is the principal means by which plants are protected in the EU and in many developing countries. The first plant variety act was enacted in 1973, and many of these countries have joined or are in the process of joining the International Union for the Protection of New Varieties of Plants (UPOV). Others, such as India, Taiwan, and Thailand, have adopted national PVP programs. While PVP certifications are considered less restrictive than patents, costs associated with application vary significantly and can be prohibitive. The application fee represents 3 percent of GDP per capita in China and Colombia and 16 percent in Kenya. The annual maintenance fee represents up to 13 percent of GDP per capita in China, 16 percent in Kenya, and 0 percent in the United States.[3]

Trade secrets are another way plants might be protected. That is, fines may be imposed if nonpublic information about plant varieties is made public. This type of protection is often sought when replication is difficult, such as with hybrids.

Trademarks and geographic designations are words or symbols used to identify novel or geographic characteristics of plant varieties to consumers—for example, Michigan cherries, Egyptian cotton, and Ethiopian coffee.

While all aforementioned forms of protection are simultaneously possible, the focus of the analysis here will be patents and PVP certifications.

DATA

Patents for innovations related to plants are prohibited in most countries in our sample. Therefore, all patent data used in this analysis are patents issued to residents of developing countries and emerging markets by the U.S. Patent and Trademark Office (USPTO). For plant patents, application data are only available from 2002. Rejection rates are calculated as the ratio of patent grants to patent applications in a given year. The rejection rate is intended to capture the quality of plant patents being issued by the United States.

Data on PVP certifications have been obtained from UPOV and the World Intellectual Property Organization (WIPO). Data on laws related to laws and agreements have been collected from the CBD, Farmers' Rights, the Food and Agriculture Organization of the U.N., WIPO, and the WTO.

Additional data, such as patents per resident and R&D expenditure as a fraction of GDP, have been gleaned from various sources to present the broader context in which decisions about plant-related intellectual property protection are being made.

EVIDENCE

Table 6.1 provides background data on the 14 developing countries and emerging markets in the sample. There is significant heterogeneity among countries for all measures: income per capita, share of agriculture in GDP, patents granted to residents per million, R&D expenditure as a fraction of GDP, and number of R&D researchers per million.

Since 1975, the quantity of plant-related innovations receiving intellectual-property rights protection has been rising in emerging markets and developing countries both at home and abroad. Figure 6.1 reports data on plant patents obtained in the United States, utility patents related to plants obtained in the United States, and PVP certifications issued in the home country. The patterns observed in the data suggest that innovations with weaker protection, PVP certifications, began to increase earlier than those seeking stronger protection through patents issued in the United States. While plant and utility patents began to rise significantly in the mid-1990s, PVP certifications began climbing significantly in the mid-1980s. Interestingly, the PVP data correspond more closely to plant and total patenting patterns in the United States, and the patent data in this sample follow plant and total plant patenting patterns in the United States with a lag of approximately 10 years.

Figure 6.2 gives data on applications for, grants of, and rejection rates for plant patents. Although patent protection of plant innovations is increasing, it is unclear whether the quality of these innovations is increasing. While the rejection rate as calculated is an imperfect measure of quality of innovations, it should give an indication of whether simply more plant-related ideas are seeking protection rather than better ideas. The high degree of variation between 2002 and 2006, the only years for which there are data, makes inference difficult. Rejection rates for all U.S. utility patents are available for a longer period and are recorded in Figure 6.3. Rejection rates were largely stable at around 60 percent in the 1990s but climbed to 70 percent by the mid-2000s.[4]

Developing countries and emerging markets have received plant-related utility patents in all subcategories. However, shares attributed to developing countries and emerging markets are relatively low in most subcategories and are largest in mushrooms, pepper, and conifers. These data appear in Figure 6.4.

For each country, we are interested in answering the following questions: Are there significant differences in intellectual-property protection sought at home and abroad? Do inventors respond to measures adopted to increase protection of plant-related ideas? Are these patterns different across countries? Figures 6.5–6.10 present data for each country in the sample and include dates of implementation of the UPOV, TRIPS, CBD, and national PVP certifications.

For Argentina and Brazil, most of the activity in IP protection of plants is in PVP certifications. In both countries, plant-related utility patents rose after 1999. Among the countries in the sample, Argentina and Israel are the earliest users of plant protection in the home country. In India and Taiwan, all the activity related to protection of plant innovations is in protection sought abroad. For Brazil, India, and Mexico, nearly all plant IP activity is concentrated in the post-TRIPS era. Following membership in UPOV, PVP certificates in Israel rose above nonzero levels consistently for more than 20 years. Of course, a formal multivariate econometric test would be warranted to ascribe causality, but the country-specific graphical analysis is suggestive.

The findings in this study are broadly consistent with the recent literature on plant-related intellectual property rights, such as Helfer (2002) and World Bank (2006). Particularly on the issue of patents,

Table 6.1 Country Data, Developing Countries, and Emerging Markets

	GDP per capita, PPP[a] $US 2005	Agriculture % GDP 2005	Patents granted to residents per million population 2005	R&D expenditure % GDP 2000–2005	Researchers in R&D per million population 1990–2005
All developing countries	1,939	11.1	—	1.02	—
East Asia and the Pacific	2,119	6.4[b,c]	—	1.61	722
Latin America and the Caribbean	4,480	8.7[d]	—	0.56	256
High income	34,759	1.7[b]	286	2.45	3,781
Middle income	2,808	9.6	—	0.85	725
Low income	610	21.4	—	0.73	—
Israel	17,828	3.0	48	4.46	—
Argentina	4,728	9.4	—	0.41	720
Chile	7,073	5.5	1	0.61	444
Costa Rica	4,627	8.7	—	0.39	—
Mexico	7,454	3.8	1	0.40	268
Brazil	4,271	8.1	1	0.98	344
Colombia	2,682	12.5	—	0.17	109
Thailand	2,750	9.9	1	0.26	287
Ecuador	2,758	6.5	—	0.07	50
Indonesia	1,302	13.4	—	0.05	207
Honduras	1,151	13.9	—	0.05	—
South Africa	5,109	2.5	—	0.76	307

| India | 736 | 18.3 | 1 | 0.85 | 119 |
| Taiwan | 16,067 | 1.7 | 1,865 | 2.26 | 3,972[e] |

[a] Purchasing power parity.

[b] 2004 data.

[c] Asia (excluding Middle East).

[d] Only Latin America.

[e] 1998–2005 data.

SOURCE: Columns 1, 2, 4, and 5: World Bank (2007); aggregates calculated from UNDP (2008). Column 3: UNDP (2008). Data on Taiwan are from Food and Fertilizer Technology Center for the Asian and Pacific Region (2008) and Taiwan Intellectual Property Office (2007). Data on population are from United Nations (2007).

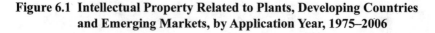

Figure 6.1 Intellectual Property Related to Plants, Developing Countries and Emerging Markets, by Application Year, 1975–2006

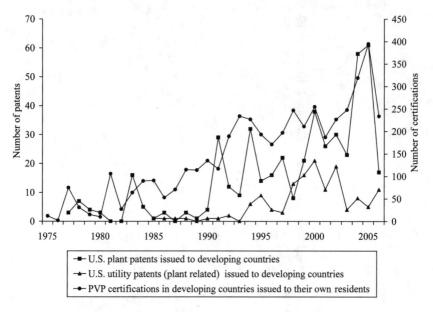

NOTE: Developing countries and emerging markets for U.S. utility and plant patents data are Israel, Costa Rica, India, South Africa, Brazil, Colombia, Argentina, Indonesia, Chile, Honduras, Mexico, Taiwan, Thailand, and Ecuador. Developing countries and emerging markets for PVP certification data are Argentina, Brazil, Chile, Colombia, Ecuador, Israel, Mexico, and South Africa. Patent origin is determined by the residence of the first-named inventor in case of U.S. plant patent and by the residence of any inventor in case of U.S. utility patent (plant related). PVP certifications are presented by grant year.

SOURCE: U.S. Plant patents, 1994–present: UPOV (2009); before 1994: Patent Technology Monitoring Team. PVP certifications, 2002–2006: UPOV (2009); 1975–2001: WIPO (n.d.). U.S. utility patents related to plants: Data retrieved by the author from the USPTO Web site: http://www.uspto.gov.

Figure 6.2 U.S. Plant Patents, Grants and Applications, Developing Countries and Emerging Markets, by Application Year, 1977–2007

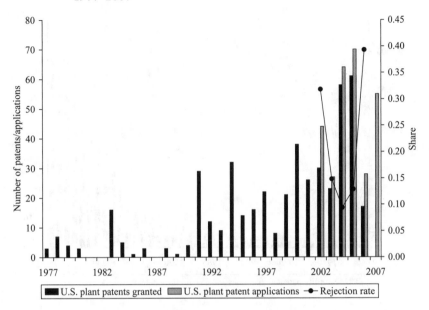

NOTE: Developing countries and emerging markets are Israel, Costa Rica, India, South Africa, Brazil, Colombia, Argentina, Indonesia, Chile, Honduras, Mexico, Taiwan, Thailand, and Ecuador.

SOURCE: Data prior to 1994: Patent Technology Monitoring Team; 1994–present: USPTO (2008a).

**Figure 6.3   U.S. Utility Patents, Grants and Applications, Developing
Countries and Emerging Markets, by Grant Year, 1965–2006**

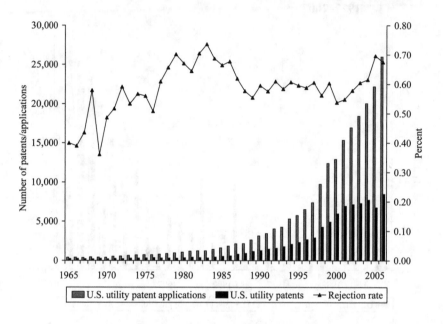

NOTE: Developing countries and emerging markets are Israel, Costa Rica, India, South
Africa, Brazil, Colombia, Argentina, Indonesia, Chile, Honduras, Mexico, Taiwan,
Thailand, and Ecuador.

SOURCE: U.S. utility patent data: USPTO (2008b). U.S. utility patent application data:
USPTO (2008c).

**Figure 6.4 U.S. Utility Patents Issued to Developing Countries and
Emerging Markets, by Plant Category, 1985–2006**

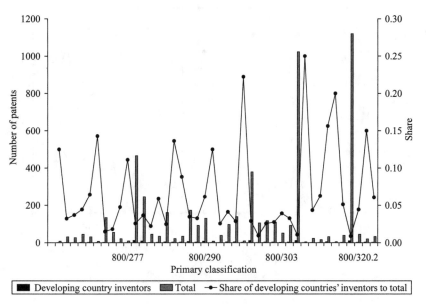

NOTE: Developing countries and emerging markets are Israel, Costa Rica, India, South
Africa, Brazil, Colombia, Argentina, Indonesia, Chile, Honduras, Mexico, Taiwan,
Thailand, and Ecuador. Patent origin is determined by the residence of at least one
inventor. Classification codes are as follows: 800/277 = Method of producing a plant
or plant part using somatic cell fusion (e.g., protoplast fusion, etc.). 800/290 = The
polynucleotide alters plant part growth (e.g., stem or tuber length, etc.). 800/303 =
Male-sterile. 800/320.2 = Rice.
SOURCE: USPTO (2008b).

Figure 6.5 Argentina, Intellectual Property, Plants, 1977–2007

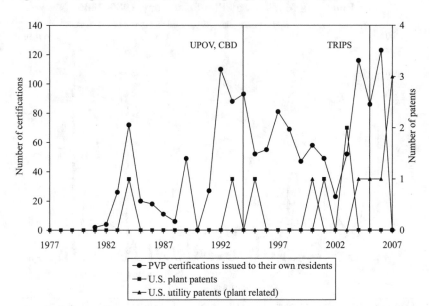

NOTE: Patent origin is determined by the residence of the first-named inventor. CBD, TRIPS, and UPOV represent the year that the country ratifies the CBD, joins the World Trade Organization, and joins UPOV. The first national Plant Variety Protection law was enacted in 1973.

SOURCE: U.S. Plant patents, 1994–present: UPOV (2009); before 1994: Patent Technology Monitoring Team. PVP certifications, 2002–2006: UPOV (2009); 1975–2001: WIPO (n.d.). U.S. utility patents related to plants: Data retrieved by the author from the USPTO Web site, http://www.uspto.gov. Law data: Summary from WIPO (2007), CBD (2009), and Farmers' Rights (2009).

Figure 6.6 Brazil, Intellectual Property, Plants, 1977–2007

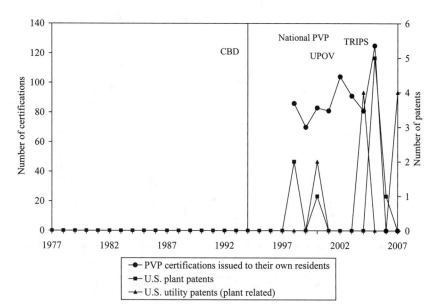

NOTE: Patent origin is determined by the residence of the first-named inventor. CBD, TRIPS, and UPOV represent the year that the country ratifies the CBD, joins the World Trade Organization, and joins UPOV. The first national Plant Variety Protection law was enacted in 1973.

SOURCE: U.S. Plant patents, 1994–present: UPOV (2009); before 1994: Patent Technology Monitoring Team. PVP certifications, 2002–2006: UPOV (2009); 1975–2001: WIPO (n.d.). U.S. utility patents related to plants: Data retrieved by the author from the USPTO Web site, http://www.uspto.gov. Law data: Summary from WIPO (2007), CBD (2009), and Farmers' Rights (2009).

Figure 6.7 India, Intellectual Property, Plants, 1977–2007

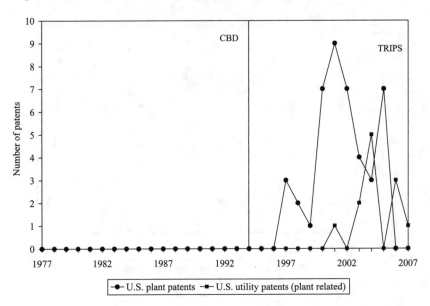

NOTE: Patent origin is determined by the residence of the first-named inventor. CBD, TRIPS, and UPOV represent the year that the country ratifies the CBD, joins the World Trade Organization, and joins UPOV. The first national Plant Variety Protection law was enacted in 1973.

SOURCE: U.S. Plant patents, 1994–present: UPOV (2009); before 1994: Patent Technology Monitoring Team. PVP certifications, 2002–2006: UPOV (2009); 1975–2001: WIPO (n.d.). U.S. utility patents related to plants: Data retrieved by the author from the USPTO Web site, http://www.uspto.gov. Law data: Summary from WIPO (2007), CBD (2009), and Farmers' Rights (2009).

Figure 6.8 Israel, Intellectual Property, Plants, 1977–2007

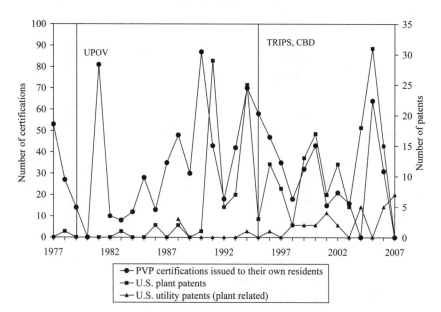

NOTE: Patent origin is determined by the residence of the first-named inventor. CBD, TRIPS, and UPOV represent the year that the country ratifies the CBD, joins the World Trade Organization, and joins UPOV. The first national Plant Variety Protection law was enacted in 1973.

SOURCE: U.S. Plant patents, 1994–present: UPOV (2009); before 1994: Patent Technology Monitoring Team. PVP certifications, 2002–2006: UPOV (2009); 1975–2001: WIPO (n.d.). U.S. utility patents related to plants: Data retrieved by the author from the USPTO Web site, http://www.uspto.gov. Law data: Summary from WIPO (2007), CBD (2009), and Farmers' Rights (2009).

Figure 6.9 Mexico, Intellectual Property, Plants, 1977–2007

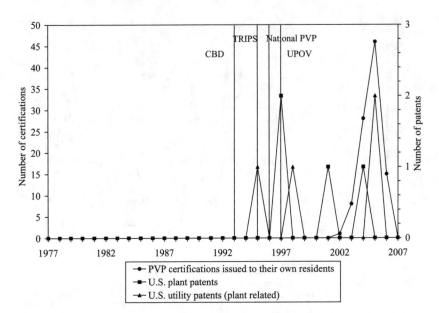

NOTE: Patent origin is determined by the residence of the first-named inventor. CBD, TRIPS, and UPOV represent the year that the country ratifies the CBD, joins the World Trade Organization, and joins UPOV. The first national Plant Variety Protection law was enacted in 1973.

SOURCE: U.S. Plant patents, 1994–present: UPOV (2009); before 1994: Patent Technology Monitoring Team. PVP certifications, 2002–2006: UPOV (2009); 1975–2001: WIPO (n.d.). U.S. utility patents related to plants: Data retrieved by the author from the USPTO Web site, http://www.uspto.gov. Law data: Summary from WIPO (2007), CBD (2009), and Farmers' Rights (2009).

Figure 6.10 Taiwan, Intellectual Property, Plants, 1977–2007

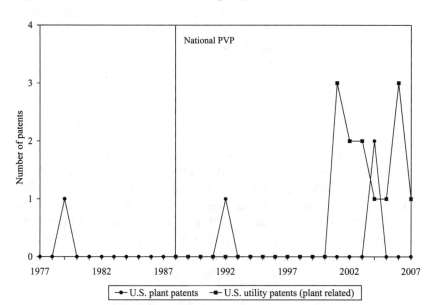

NOTE: Patent origin is determined by the residence of the first-named inventor. CBD, TRIPS, and UPOV represent the year that the country ratifies the CBD, joins the World Trade Organization, and joins UPOV. The first national Plant Variety Protection law was enacted in 1973.

SOURCE: U.S. Plant patents, 1994–present: UPOV (2009); before 1994: Patent Technology Monitoring Team. PVP certifications, 2002–2006: UPOV (2009); 1975–2001: WIPO (n.d.). U.S. utility patents related to plants: Data retrieved by the author from the USPTO Web site, http://www.uspto.gov. Law data: Summary from WIPO (2007), CBD (2009), and Farmers' Rights (2009).

the conventional wisdom is that developing countries prefer weaker IP rights and that these will spur innovation. This analysis suggests that a more nuanced and time-series investigation of the empirical record is in order and that the issue is not settled.

CONCLUSION

An examination of data on intellectual property related to plants finds that there is increased activity in protecting intellectual property in and by developing countries. This finding implies that foreign patent offices are complements in most countries. In Brazil, India, and Mexico, there is a noticeable TRIPS effect, and protected inventions increase at home and abroad after TRIPS passage in 1997. From the data it is difficult to glean implications for taking advantage of new biofuel opportunities, for example, beyond protection of ideas. Were these preexisting ideas or new ideas seeking protection? Did new knowledge arise as a result of new protection or in spite of it? What are the results with respect to commercialization? This is still an open research question and deserves further attention in future research.

Notes

The author is grateful to seminar participants at the Werner Sichel Lecture Series at Western Michigan University and in the Department of Economics at Michigan State University. Excellent research assistance by Chaleampong Kongcharoen is also acknowledged.

1. The scope of per se patents is not only the application identified but applications not yet identified.
2. USPTO definition, http://www.uspto.gov/web/offices/pac/plant/.
3. World Bank (2006), UNDP (2008), and author's calculations. GDP per capita data are for 2005.
4. One must be careful in interpreting the data on rejection rates, as applications and rejections arrive at irregular and different intervals.

References

Council for Economic Planning and Development (CEPD). 2007. *Taiwan Statistical Data Book 2007*. http://www.cepd.gov.tw/encontent/m1.aspx?sNo= 0008371&key=&ex=%20&ic=&cd= (accessed February 7, 2010). Taipei, Taiwan: CEPD.

Farmers' Rights. 2009. "Legislation and Policy Database." http://www .farmersrights.org/database/index.html (accessed August 25, 2009). Lysaker, Norway: Farmer's Rights.

Finger, J. Michael. 2004. "Poor People's Knowledge." World Bank Policy Research Paper Series No. 3205. Washington, DC: World Bank.

Food and Agriculture Organization of the United Nations (FAO). "Legal Office." 2009. http://faolex.fao.org (accessed August 25, 2009). Rome: FAO.

Food and Fertilizer Technology Center for the Asian and Pacific Region. 2008. *Agricultural Statistics 2007*. http://www.agnet.org/situationer/stats/21.html (accessed January 23, 2010). Taipei, Taiwan: FFTASPAC.

International Union for the Protection of New Varieties of Plants, Plant Variety Protection Certifications (UPOV). 2009. "Plant Variety Protection Statistics for the Period 2004–2008." http://www.upov.int/en/publications/statistics .htm (accessed January 23, 2010). Geneva: UPOV.

Nogués, J. J. 1993. "Social Costs and Benefits of Introducing Patent Protection for Pharmaceutical Drugs in Developing Countries." *Developing Economies* 31(1): 24–53.

Taiwan Intellectual Property Office. 2007. http://www.tipo.gov.tw (accessed October 2008). Taipei, Taiwan: Taiwan Intellectual Property Office.

U.N. Convention on Biological Diversity (CBD). 2009. "List of Parties." http://www.cbd.int/convention/parties/list/ (accessed August 25, 2009).

U.N., Department of Economic and Social Affairs, Population Division. 2007. *World Population Prospects 1950–2050: The 2006 Revision Database*. New York: United Nations. http://esa.un.org/unpp (accessed August 26, 2009).

U.N. Development Programme. 2008. *Human Development Indices: A Statistical Update–2008 Rankings*. http://hdrstats.undp.org (accessed January 23, 2010). New York: U.N. Development Programme.

U.S. Patent and Trademark Office (USPTO). 2008a. "Plant Patents Report." ftp://ftp.uspto.gov/pub/taf/plant.htm (accessed November 10, 2010). Alexandria, VA: USPTO.

———. 2008b. "Number of Utility Patent Applications Filed in the United States, by Country of Origin, Calendar Years 1965 to Present." http://www .uspto.gov/web/offices/ac/ido/oeip/taf/appl_yr.htm (accessed November 10, 2010). Alexandria, VA: USPTO.

————. 2008c. "Extended Year Set—Historic Patents by Country, State, and Year Utility Patents (December 2008)." http://www.uspto.gov/web/offices/ ac/ido/oeip/taf/cst_utlh.htm (accessed November 10, 2010). Alexandria, VA: USPTO.

World Bank. 2006. *Intellectual Property Rights: Designing Regimes to Support Plant Breeding in Developing Countries*. Washington, DC: The World Bank.

————. 2007. "World Development Indicators 2007." http://go.worldbank .org/3JU2HA60D0 (accessed January 23, 2010). Washington, DC: World Bank.

World Intellectual Property Organization (WIPO). 2007. "Patents Granted by Office, 1985–2005." http://wipo.int/ipstats/en/statistics/patents/ (accessed February 7, 2010). Geneva: WIPO.

————. n.d. "Statistics on Plant Varieties." http://www.wipo.int/ipstats/en/ statistics/plants (accessed August 2009). Geneva: WIPO.

World Trade Organization. 2009. "TRIPS News." http://www.wto.org/english/ tratop_e/trips_e/trips_e.htm (accessed February 7, 2010). Geneva: WTO.

7

The Challenges and Opportunities of Twenty-First-Century Global Markets

Hadi Salehi Esfahani
University of Illinois at Urbana-Champaign

Are we preparing our younger generations for the challenges and opportunities of the twenty-first-century global markets? As markets become increasingly global, tough competition for every skill is emerging from around the world. But fascinating opportunities are also being formed to serve people in different corners of the globe in new ways. Are we, as a society and as individuals, developing the right skills and procedures to deal with the upcoming challenges and to take advantage of the new global opportunities? Or are we about to see our jobs outsourced and our lives face greater uncertainty?

These are critical questions that all of us living in the early twenty-first century have to grapple with, one way or another. Global trends have come to matter in significant ways in our career choices and business decisions, as well as government policies that we advocate. To think through these issues and to make informed choices as professionals and citizens, we need to have a basic understanding of the main forces behind global market dynamics. The literature on globalization offers many perspectives that highlight such forces from different angles. This chapter brings together a host of those perspectives and makes new observations regarding the current and future globalization trends. To start the discussion, it is useful to briefly review the key trends and lessons from the past.

105

PAST GLOBALIZATION TRENDS

The most notable forces behind globalization are improvements in transportation and information technologies that have brought different parts of the world into closer contact with each other. This has enabled companies in each country to see the world market within their reach and to think globally when choosing what processes to keep inside the firm, where to locate, and which processes to outsource domestically or internationally. Such considerations are not just for large corporations such as Caterpillar or Archer Daniels Midland. Small firms and individuals also need to be aware of their positions in global markets. Many industries, such as auto parts, have long been involved in that process. More recently, many products and services that previously enjoyed natural protection in each locality, such as retail sales, have come to face a much wider competition.

Technology, however, is not the entire story behind globalization. Government policies and institutional developments have also played major roles. Even decades ago, when transportation and communications costs were high, they were often minor compared to the myriad of barriers erected by governments to protect domestic industry or to generate rents and collect revenue. Those barriers have markedly declined since World War II. Government action has also mattered in terms of streamlining domestic regulation, law and order, and control of corruption and extortion (or security of property rights in general). Globalization would not have been possible without expanding public support for liberal trade and without increasing government ability to invest in public goods and to bring order, efficiency, and security to domestic markets.

What accounts for the change in public attitudes and the improvement in government capabilities? Concerning attitudes toward trade policy, the important factors have been improvements in the operation of labor and capital markets and the expansion of social insurance mechanisms such as unemployment insurance and social security. These factors have mattered because they have reduced the costs of external shocks on domestic producers. Under liberal trade, innovations and entries and exits in global markets often force local producers to respond and compete or go out of business. In either case, access to efficient sources of credit and insurance can reduce the costs imposed on local firms and workers and enable them to withstand external shocks, adjusting to them or moving to new localities and lines of business where they can compete more effectively. The enhanced efficiency of capital and labor markets and the expansion of social insurance over the past several decades have eased such adjustments and account for the increased palatability of liberal trade policies, especially in more advanced countries. Lack of similar developments in many poor regions of the world has either prevented governments from opening up trade or has rendered local industries vulnerable to external shocks, impeding investment and causing hardship for large parts of the population. For similar reasons, the pre-WWII free trade under colonial rule did not bring much prosperity to the Third World.

This discussion raises the question of why many countries have managed to improve their governance and make globalization possible. Note that this is a central question because the developments in market institutions and technology ultimately depend on the capabilities of the government to establish an enabling environment for innovation and exchange. Also, it so happens that the full answer to this question has remained elusive. In fact, if we had a complete answer to this question, we could devise solutions to governance problems of all countries, and underdevelopment would be a problem of the past. Of course, we do have some insights regarding the sources of good governance in parts of the world. But our knowledge remains limited, and that is a major reason why spreading good governance has met with limited success.

We know that good governance ultimately requires constraints on arbitrary rule, that is, separation of powers and checks and balances. We also know that there must be mechanisms to aggregate the demands and information of individuals and interest groups regarding what needs to be achieved through government policy. In addition, there must be procedures for assessing the performance of policymakers and rewarding them based on their success in delivering socially desirable policies. However, we don't know which sets of rules and institutions can ensure these goals in each society and what the necessary steps are to implement them if the country has not already found a solution. In fact, progress in most societies has been made mostly through experiments and accidental discovery rather than fully analyzed designs. Typically, the process has started with periods of massive uprising against arbitrary or foreign rulers. The new institutions that have come about in those ways have often proved to be inadequate, either resulting in deterioration in governance or prompting further change. In some cases, such as with the United States, the vision of the leaders and the constellation of forces at the time have produced valuable and lasting results. In other situations, such as in Cambodia in the 1970s, the uprising has replaced one inadequate regime with another, far more arbitrary and destructive one.

The difficulty societies have in attaining good governance lies in the complexity of the problems that they face. The governance rules and policies that work in each society must match a myriad of elements that comprise the society's economic resources, culture, religion, group affiliations, and identities. For example, decentralization seems to have been a very positive force in China's impressive economic growth. But in an economically underdeveloped, fragmented, and partially tribal society such as Pakistan, decentralization may strengthen clannish social relations that impede education and infrastructure and thereby deny most of the population the benefits of integration into national and global markets.

Another major problem in reforming governance is the massive coordination effort that it requires: An overwhelming majority of the population must be convinced that the new rules being adopted are likely to work and that everyone else shares the view that such a consensus exists. This requirement also poses a dilemma: broad coordination often needs to be reached with the help of a charismatic leader or a well-organized group. Once in the coordinator position, the leader or the group may come to control the system and have the option to impose certain rules. This could defeat the purpose of the initial movement to bring about change. However, in some contexts, the dictatorship of the coordinator can be crucial in achieving reform, as in Korea, Taiwan, and Singapore, where the heavy hand of the ruling politicians in the initial stages has been associated with spectacular takeoffs. Absence of effective coordination, on the other hand, could undermine economic growth, as shown with the sharp drop in Indonesia's economic growth after democratization in 1998 has shown. Note that these examples also suggest that in an underdeveloped country, governance improvement may come about under dictatorship, even though eventually economic development requires democratization. These observations, together with the fact that the conditions of each society are complex and constantly subject to change, highlight the reasons why governance reform has been so difficult in many countries and has remained an art rather than a science.

Despite the difficulties in improving governance, there has been a gradual process of reform in a large part of the world, which has in turn facilitated international exchanges and has ushered in the current globalization episode. This process and its concomitant technological and attitude changes have furthermore mounted pressure on other countries to change and adapt. When a country such as Myanmar does not respond, it becomes isolated and loses out on the tremendous benefits that interaction with the rest of the world can offer. But simple responses, such as opening domestic markets to international trade, do not solve the problem either. Yemen's economy, for example, has virtually stagnated since its trade liberalization in the mid-1990s. The government has been waiting for a surge in private investment to create jobs and motivate the young to acquire education and skills, but the private sector has focused on imports rather than domestic production, doubting that the government's policies would produce a skilled labor force and a buoyant demand for domestic goods. In any event, the challenges of globalization have increased the urgency of finding solutions to local economic and governance failures in all countries, and there is increasing realization that solutions need to be tailored to the specific conditions at the national and subnational levels.

Although tailoring solutions may seem a reasonable and straightforward point, applying it in practice has not been easy for international organizations. A vivid example of this was the response of the International Monetary Fund (IMF) to a financial crisis in East Asia. In the 1990s, many East Asian countries had followed the advice of the IMF and opened up their economies to international finance. But due to regulatory weaknesses, many of those countries had attracted too much short-term foreign capital. When signs of economic weakness appeared in some of those economies in 1997–1998, foreign lenders withdrew their money and asset markets in East Asia collapsed. The solution to the problem should have been foreign support for regulatory reform in banking and finance, with governments maintaining their expenditures and allowing their deficits to rise as a means of cushioning the shock for the local population. The IMF offered assistance but conditioned it on governments cutting their expenditures and bringing unnecessary hardship to those economies. The reason for the IMF's condition was its past experience in many other developing countries where government deficits themselves had been a major culprit in causing or deepening financial crises. However, those conditions did not apply to East Asian countries in 1997–1998. The IMF failed to adjust its policies to specific conditions for three main reasons: 1) the situation was complex, and the right solution was not entirely obvious at the time; 2) allowing for variation in IMF policies would have opened the door to demands for exceptions in other cases where fiscal adjustment is indeed crucial; and 3) since IMF managers did not believe that their organization could easily sort out different cases, they must have felt that allowing for variation could undermine the IMF's internal discipline.

The need for diversity of solutions across places has posed a problem for global markets. It has meant that in the economic game, the world is not completely flat, as Thomas Friedman (2005) would suggest. Labor regulations, for example, have to take account of local circumstances in terms of social and family structure, formal insurance options, work habits, legal systems, etc. Similarly, environmental regulations have reflected the priorities of the populations across places and their abilities to turn their concerns into policies. Multilateral organizations such as the IMF and the World Bank tried to devise uniform recommendations to facilitate their own decision-making processes, and multinationals have shown preference for uniform and permissive regulations that reduce their costs of operation. But the people in many localities have been reluctant or unable to adapt, resulting in an uneven distribution of global economic activity.

To sum up, the past trends in globalization have consisted of greater integration of world markets with the help of technological progress and policy changes across countries. However, the result has been uneven, with or without efforts to impose uniform solutions. The question is, what should we expect for the trends in the coming decades given what we know about the past?

THE COMING TRENDS

In the past, while technological developments have generally contributed to increased integration of world markets, institutional factors —basic norms and rules such as culture and constitution—have not always been as supportive. Also, technologies embodied in physical capital have been relatively easy to transfer across countries, whereas the replication of institutions and intangible technologies such as management has faced greater obstacles. However, there is increasing realization among policy analysts as well as policymakers the world over that some essential lessons from each country's experience must be transferable to others if careful attention is paid to the conditions and nuances. The consequences of this realization will likely set the trends in globalization during the coming decades. Cross-country lessons will be increasingly distilled to arrive at general messages, along with a host of ifs and buts and examples for potential application in specific circumstances. This is likely to yield more practical ideas for governance reform with minimal risk, hence further lowering the institutional barriers to globalization.

The policy reforms of the coming decades are *unlikely* to make countries uniform in terms of governance and regulation, but they will bring about greater harmony. They will enable countries to participate in global processes and cooperate in establishing effective international treaties and organizations that enhance fair and broad competition. At the same time, diversity in institutions and regulatory systems is likely to remain. Although this may entail some costs for business, it will also serve as a source of strength for the global economy. Country differences can increase the range of options available in terms of products and processes, allowing better potential fit between production requirements and consumers. Indeed, markets will reaffirm their great ability to bring harmony to the diverse set of actors working differentiated conditions. And this will increase the resilience of the world economy in the face of unforeseen shocks, for exactly the same reasons that diversity in biology ensures longevity of species.

As the means to establish and harmonize situation-specific solutions proliferate, decentralization will become a more tangible reality for larger parts of the world. There will also be greater demands for and materialization of deeper democratic rule. These and all other reforms and adaptations at the local level are likely to strengthen and broaden the participation of national and subnational governments in forming the institutions of global governance (such as the United Nations, the World Trade Organization, the IMF, the World Bank, the Bank of International Settlements, and the World Court). Rather than preaching uniformity, as the World Bank and IMF have often done in the past, international institutions will increasingly move toward a role parallel to that of markets: bringing harmony to a diverse set of players.

How will governments and markets deal with our current concerns about globalization? To explore the possible answers to this question, let's start with the outsourcing issue, which has caused some anxiety in recent years for workers and professionals in many countries. This also happens to.be among the easiest issues to address. To understand the reason, first note that outsourcing will be going in all directions. So, if some jobs are lost in the United States and outsourced to countries where they can be done relatively more cheaply, there must also be other tasks that are relatively more expensive in those countries and can be outsourced to the United States. Would this type of global competition press down the U.S. wages and salaries toward those currently prevailing in India or China? Not if American workers win the competition in their fields of specialization because of their productivity and high quality of their services. Of course, this cannot happen in all lines of economic activity. So, over time, part of the American labor force may have to shift to new jobs as its comparative advantage is redefined by global markets. Continued improvements in the labor market will reduce the costs associated with the shift, and the remaining burden is likely to be cushioned with the help of well-functioning private capital and insurance markets, as well as social insurance mechanisms. Similar trends will also be taking place in the rest of the world. In many developing countries, where the costs of adjustment have been falling mostly on labor, there will be further institution building to diminish the hardships and share the risks. All of these effects will soften the opposition to liberal trade around the world and thereby deepen globalization.

Another current concern about globalization is the rising inequality. Globalization has increased the returns to skills and, as a result, has widened the gap between the rich and the poor. This is parallel to the effects of technological and institutional changes, which have in fact been much stronger forces behind the increased inequality. These forces will continue raising the rewards to skills, largely because ultimately that is how they help incomes rise. However, the level and composition of skills are likely to change, enabling a much larger share of the labor force to take advantage of opportunities presented by globalization and new technologies. The enhanced abilities of the governments will also bring about more efficient, situation-specific labor regulations that expand rewarding job opportunities for broader segments of the population around the world. These factors should jointly help to stop or even to reverse the recent trends in inequality.

Of course, for the enhancement and expansion in skills to take place, there must be major reforms in education (especially curricula and teaching methods) to facilitate the acquisition of the relevant skills. There will be better ways to condense information in various fields and pass them on to students, along with more general skills of communications and critical thinking. Like many other reforms, at the moment we may not know the exact solutions that will come about in different contexts, but our efforts to improve knowledge in this area and to experiment with possible solutions are likely to bear fruit over the coming decades.

Could the rise in global incomes be thwarted by the exhaustion of natural resources on earth? While that is a possibility, it is by no means a likely outcome. The incentives to find renewable and expandable substitutes for exhaustible resources are getting stronger. There are already such substitutes available for many natural resources, though they are not always used widely due to cost or safety consideration (such as nuclear energy, which can be a substitute for petroleum). Another factor that makes the picture more hopeful is the shift in the pattern of production and consumption toward products that use fewer natural resources per dollar of their value. This trend is most vivid in the rising role of services in the economy, which require substantially less energy than manufacturing and agriculture. Similar trends, combined with institutional reforms in developing countries, are likely to address the environmental concerns of expanding production around the globe.

Similar responses and trends should be expected in the case of many other problems associated with globalization. The overall picture seems to be a hopeful one, largely based on the ability of the world community to overcome the most pressing obstacle to its economic prosperity at present, which is lack of sufficient knowledge and ability to spread good practices in governance, regulation, and market development.

WHAT COMBINATIONS OF SKILLS DO WE NEED IN THE TWENTY-FIRST CENTURY?

There will be no shortage of decent jobs in the coming decades. To enjoy a prosperous life, people need, among other things, good shelter, food, medical care, education, and entertainment. Those who deliver these products need to identify the demands and satisfy them with high standards and low costs. To achieve this, they need high-quality and cost-effective inputs, which must be produced by others, who in turn depend on each other's products and services.[1] An important part of the inputs needed at every stage is the innovative know-how to perform tasks more effectively and improve the output. Furthermore, those who provide such inputs will need the services of others who offer research and advice on how innovation processes can themselves be made more effective and innovative. At every stage, there is also a need for individuals who can facilitate the transactions and make them more reliable. Finally, there is a need for people who study the global system of transactions at broader levels and help make it more effective. It is evident that in its entirety, this chain is very complex and, with globalization, spans the entire world economy, involving billions of jobs. Each of those jobs can be made more productive and remunerative, which will benefit the jobholders as well as all others who interact with them as buyers or sellers.

In this context, the skills that one can acquire and use productively in each country depend on the production processes already in place and the institutional capabilities of that country. For example, in the past, the conditions in the United States enabled it to lead in the development of new knowledge, technologies, and products (ranging from scientific and industrial equipment to music and cinema). This position is likely to be maintained in the first half of the twenty-first century, and the skills most rewarded will be those that contribute to innovations. Of course, competition will increase around the world. But as the numbers of those involved in the process rise, there will be room for greater specialization and focus on narrower areas where leadership can be maintained, with some of the activities being passed on to other countries that can perform them more effectively. This will make the jobs more productive in the United States and in other countries, raising incomes here and abroad.

Finally, to be effective in our jobs, we need to specialize in the tasks that we take up, communicate effectively with those who interact with us, and develop a practical and reasonably good understanding of the big picture of the global economy. At the same time, we must maintain some flexibility to be able to redefine our positions, learn new skills, and switch to new tasks as our sources of comparative advantage shift over time. This requires a combination of quantitative and technical knowledge as well as communication and business skills. Many of the specialized skills may be learned on the job or at the graduate level. In pregraduate stages of education, we need to learn a great deal of relatively general math and sciences as well as social sciences and humanities. And, of course, in all these areas, our knowledge must include broad perspectives on where things stand globally.

Note

1. For example, to paint the rooms in your house, you need a painter to do a neat job while spending a minimal amount of time. This depends on the skills and incentives of the painter, as well as the equipment and the quality of paints she can use. In particular, she needs durable brushes and painting equipment that spread paint quickly and consistently. Producing such equipment and material in turn requires use of appropriate inputs and the application of scientific and industrial innovations, which are produced by others, and so on and so forth.

Reference

Friedman, Thomas. 2005. *The World Is Flat: A Brief History of the Twenty-First Century.* New York: Farrar, Straus, and Giroux.

The Authors

Sisay Asefa is a professor of economics at Western Michigan University.

Lisa D. Cook is an assistant professor of economics at James Madison College, Michigan State University.

Hadi Salehi Esfahani is a professor of economics at the University of Illinois at Urbana-Champaign.

Ian Goldin is a professorial fellow at Balliol College and director of the James Martin 21st Century School, University of Oxford.

Joseph P. Joyce is a professor of economics at Wellesley College.

Susan Pozo is a professor of economics at Western Michigan University.

Kenneth A. Reinert is a professor of public policy at George Mason University.

Linda Tesar is a professor and chair of the Department of Economics at the University of Michigan.

Index

The italic letters *f, n,* and *t* following a page number indicate that the subject information of the heading is within a figure, note, or table, respectively, on that page. Double italics indicate multiple but consecutive elements.

About the Institute

The W.E. Upjohn Institute for Employment Research is a nonprofit research organization devoted to finding and promoting solutions to employment-related problems at the national, state, and local levels. It is an activity of the W.E. Upjohn Unemployment Trustee Corporation, which was established in 1932 to administer a fund set aside by Dr. W.E. Upjohn, founder of The Upjohn Company, to seek ways to counteract the loss of employment income during economic downturns.

The Institute is funded largely by income from the W.E. Upjohn Unemployment Trust, supplemented by outside grants, contracts, and sales of publications. Activities of the Institute comprise the following elements: 1) a research program conducted by a resident staff of professional social scientists; 2) a competitive grant program, which expands and complements the internal research program by providing financial support to researchers outside the Institute; 3) a publications program, which provides the major vehicle for disseminating the research of staff and grantees, as well as other selected works in the field; and 4) an Employment Management Services division, which manages most of the publicly funded employment and training programs in the local area.

The broad objectives of the Institute's research, grant, and publication programs are to 1) promote scholarship and experimentation on issues of public and private employment and unemployment policy, and 2) make knowledge and scholarship relevant and useful to policymakers in their pursuit of solutions to employment and unemployment problems.

Current areas of concentration for these programs include causes, consequences, and measures to alleviate unemployment; social insurance and income maintenance programs; compensation; workforce quality; work arrangements; family labor issues; labor-management relations; and regional economic development and local labor markets.